BEHIND THE BLUE AND GRAY

THE SOLDIER'S LIFE IN THE CIVIL WAR

The Civil War was not simply a contest between fighting men. Often the outcome of battles was decided far from the front in the factories that produced these rows of cannons and fleets of ships. With weapons stockpiles such as this, the North's industrial strength eventually overwhelmed the poorly equipped South.

BEHIND THE BLUE AND GRAY

THE SOLDIER'S LIFE IN THE CIVIL WAR

DELIA RAY

SCHOLASTIC INC.
New York Toronto London Auckland Sydney

Front cover illustration: *News from Home*, Eleanor S. Brockenbrough Library, The Museum of the Confederacy, Richmond, Virginia

Back cover photo: The Library of Congress

ISBN 0-590-46839-1

Copyright © 1991 by Laing Communications Inc. All rights reserved. Published by Scholastic Inc., 555 Broadway, New York, NY 10012, by arrangement with Lodestar Books, an affiliate of Dutton Children's Books, a division of Penguin Books USA Inc.

12 11 10 9 8 7 6 5 4 3 2 1   4 5 6 7 8 9/9

Printed in the U.S.A.   34

First Scholastic printing, March 1994

for RFR,
who will wear
stars in her crown

Contents

Acknowledgments

I am especially grateful to Bobby Ray and Carolyn Clark for their generous editorial guidance. I would also like to thank Brian Pohanka for his expert review of the manuscript, John Leib for his willingness to send photographs at a moment's notice, and George Hobart at the Library of Congress for his patience in unearthing hard-to-find images.

When they marched through the streets of New York on their way to war, the Federal soldiers of the Seventh New York Regiment knew very little of what lay ahead. Swept along by the fanfare, most were too excited to be frightened. They happily waved to the crowd and craned their necks to see the city draped in banners and flags.

ONE

Wakening to War

On April 19, 1861, Theodore Winthrop marched through the streets of New York City and left his quiet life behind. One week earlier peace had finally crumbled in America. Southerners had cut all ties with their northern countrymen by firing the first shot of the Civil War. Now President Abraham Lincoln was calling for volunteers to join the Union Army and defend the nation against the "southern rebels." Winthrop, a shy, thin man, with bright eyes and wavy hair, was one of the first men in the North to answer Lincoln's call.

Before the war, Winthrop spent his days writing poetry and novels. But even for a talented author, it was difficult to describe the scene in New York on that sunny afternoon in 1861. Thousands of people flooded the streets to watch the soldiers of New York's Seventh Regiment march off to Washington, D.C., where they would fight to stop the Southerners from capturing the nation's capital. As Private Winthrop later wrote, "It was worth a life that march."

Line after line of soldiers dressed in spotless uniforms paraded down Broadway, their bayonets shining in the sun. From his place among the troops, Winthrop could barely hear the blaring military band above the roaring crowd that stretched for two miles. Hand-kerchiefs floated down like snow from the windows and rooftops, where ladies looked out on the parting men with tears in their eyes. As Winthrop passed through the crowd, proud citizens slapped him on the back and offered him gifts—pocketknives, combs, cigars, slippers, sandwiches, and fruit. The event seemed more like a victory parade than a march to war.

While men worried about the dangers ahead and many women wept to see their sons and husbands go, the city was swept up in the spirit of success. The most dashing members of New York society had joined the famous Seventh Regiment—young men from wealthy families and fine backgrounds. Most of the volunteers had never fired a gun in battle, camped outdoors for any length of time, or endured the hardships of army life. But in the spring of 1861, none of that seemed to matter. Winthrop and the men of the Seventh were so sure of victory that they volunteered to serve in the army for only thirty days. They fully expected to end the war with one winning battle and be home again in a single month's time.

When the snappy Seventh reached Washington, D.C., the regiment was welcomed with more celebrations. The citizens of the capital were overwhelmed with relief. They had feared that enemy forces from surrounding southern states would strike at any moment. Now a precious supply of one thousand Union soldiers had finally arrived to defend against an attack. Tromping past the cheering spectators, the New Yorkers headed directly for the White House, where President Lincoln came out to wave to them. As one aide commented, the relieved president "smiled all over."

As the new recruits waited for further orders, life in Washington fulfilled their grand expectations of soldiering. Since there were no army barracks in the city, the troops camped in the formal chambers of the Capitol Building. At night hundreds of soldiers sprawled throughout the crimson and gold halls of Congress, sleeping underneath the desks or draped across the plush sofas. As soon as the sound of bugles echoed through the building in the morning, the Capitol became a huge playground. The soldiers in the balconies shouted playful insults at the men below, who hooted back louder replies. Recruits leaped to the platform reserved for leaders of Congress, delivered rowdy speeches, and sang songs.

A volunteer says good-bye to his family while members of his regiment wait outside. Some soldiers did not see their wives or children during the entire four-year struggle.

Eventually the soldiers headed out to a nearby park to practice marching and handling their weapons. But even the long hours of military drill were pleasant. Pink cherry blossoms filled the park with the smell of spring. During breaks from drilling, the men marched down the hill to dine at the big hotels or stretched out on the shady lawn to watch the other regiments at work.

Every day more and more Federal troops poured into the city. "It seemed," observed Private Winthrop, "as if all the able-bodied men in the country were moving, on the first of May . . . to agreeable, but dusty lodgings on the Potomac [River]."

Most of the other volunteers did not look as polished and soldierly as the men of the Seventh Regiment. In fact, from a glance at their uniforms, it appeared as though many were members of completely different armies. The official battle dress for the Union Army consisted of dark blue coats and dark or light blue trousers, but very few volunteers reported for service in this outfit. The Minnesota recruits marched into Washington looking like lumberjacks with their red flannel shirts and black trousers. Some soldiers from Vermont who could not afford weapons or standard uniforms simply appeared for duty in their everyday clothes. Several groups of volunteers called Zouaves wore baggy red pants and red caps with tassels. Even the Seventh Regiment soldiers, who looked so proper in their trim gray uniforms, had chosen the wrong color. Gray was the official color of the southern army.

The Federal recruits also differed in their reasons for joining the army. When Private Winthrop made his decision to volunteer, he announced, "I go to put an end to slavery." For him, war was a mission to halt the southern practice of holding blacks in bondage. Yet few northern soldiers thought like Winthrop. Most cared more about the money they would earn for enlisting than the hardships of the slaves. The war came during depressed times in the North, when it was difficult to find work. By volunteering, a private could make $13 a month for his services—a small sum, but better than nothing at all. In addition to wages, the army offered an opportunity for excitement and adventure. Many young men had never traveled past the outskirts of their hometowns. Now was their chance to see the mysterious world beyond. But whether they joined the army to travel or to avoid being called a coward, most Federal soldiers shared one common goal: to preserve the Union.

In the South, men were just as eager to fight. About the same time Winthrop marched through the streets of New York, a boisterous crowd of young southern men gathered in Virginia to shout their support for a split from the North. It was early in the morning when cheers rang out at the University of Virginia. A group of students had spotted a new flag flying from the tallest building on campus. The flag represented the Confederate States of America, the nation created by unhappy Southerners who wanted independence from the Union.

A nineteen-year-old named Randolph McKim was one of the

students who had climbed to the top of the building after midnight to hang the Confederate flag. Like most young men at the university, McKim could not concentrate on his studies in the spring of 1861. It was impossible to think of mathematics and philosophy when battles were brewing nearby. Professors struggled

In the early days before defeats in Virginia daunted their confidence, the Federals reveled in the relaxed and pleasant atmosphere of camp. Here, several officers enjoy a picnic outside their tent and smoke tobacco, one of the soldiers' favorite pastimes during the Civil War. The young officer with the dog is Lieutenant George Armstrong Custer, who later earned notoriety as a bold, controversial general in the Civil War and in Indian battles.

to maintain order in their classes, but their efforts were useless. When the students heard the commotion over the Confederate flag outside, they stampeded out of their classrooms to join the excitement.

Out on the lawn a crowd gathered under the flag to hear several students speak out against the North and urge others to fight for independence. "The Union leaders in Washington, D.C., want to destroy the South," the young men declared. "We must stop them from taking control of our laws and our economy." The students did not focus on the issue of slavery in their speeches. Just as most Northerners did not join the army to end slavery, most Southerners did not join just to protect it. The majority of families in the South could not even afford to own slaves. But these citizens believed that much more than slavery was at stake.

In mid-April, when President Lincoln called forth 75,000 volunteers to suppress the rebellion, Southerners were convinced that their fears were coming true. The Union Army was ready to invade—to overrun their land, storm their homes, and wipe out their traditions. People no longer needed to hear persuasive speeches. All across the South, men rushed to the cities and town squares to enlist in the Confederate Army.

The main worry of the volunteers was not whether they might lose their lives, but whether they would reach the battleground before the fighting was over. "So impatient did I become for starting," wrote one young volunteer from Arkansas, "that I felt like ten thousand pins were pricking me in every part of my body."

The excited recruits ignored the fact that their army possessed far fewer men and supplies than the enemy. They were certain that they would make better soldiers than the Northerners, who many thought came from a land of big cities and easy living. Nearly two-thirds of the Confederate Army were farmers, accustomed to using guns, living outdoors, and working at jobs that tested strength and endurance. One southern recruit summed up the beliefs of most of his fellow soldiers when he wrote in a letter, "You need not be alarmed about me, my dear mother; there is some danger in case of battle, but very little; the Yankees cannot shoot." The volunteers were so full of confidence that they created boastful names for their military companies—the Barbour

County Yankee Hunters, the Cherokee Lincoln Killers, the Dixie Heroes.

Randolph McKim was anxious to join his friends and rush to war. But there was one dark thought that made him pause: He did not want to disappoint his father. McKim's family lived in Maryland, a state that lay on the border between the North and the South and remained bitterly torn between Union and Confederate supporters. Although McKim and his father were strongly devoted to each other, they clashed in their views about the war. The older man, who remained loyal to the Union, tried desperately to convince his son to give up the Confederate cause. Finally, Randolph McKim promised not to join the southern army without his father's consent.

But soon the torture of watching his fellow students leave for the battlefront without him grew unbearable. When exams at the university had ended, McKim headed for Maryland to plead once again for his parents' permission to fight for the Confederacy. On the way he visited a southern regiment that was stationed nearby. McKim felt embarrassed when he saw his old classmates in uniform, their faces already tanned from camp life. His own face was as white as paper, and he felt awkward in his everyday clothes.

At that moment McKim decided to break his promise to his parents. After writing them a letter to explain his plans, he set out to enlist in the First Maryland Regiment, which many of his hometown friends and relatives had joined. Within ten days, he found himself marching toward battle at Manassas, Virginia, listening to the thundering of cannon grow louder. McKim never spoke with his father again; the older man died before the war ended, still declaring loyalty to the government that his son opposed.

In Washington, D.C., the Union troops received their orders to begin the march for Manassas on July 16. In three months the Union Army had swelled to an enormous size. The Seventh Regiment recruits boarded trains back to New York when their thirty days of service were over, but there were plenty of three-month volunteers to take their place. Now 35,000 soldiers were crammed into the city, restlessly waiting for the trumpets to signal their army to rumble forward.

The mismatch of uniforms on both sides had serious consequences. At Bull Run, when an officer mistook a Confederate regiment dressed in blue for Federal troops, Federal Captain Charles Griffin was ordered to hold fire. By the time the error was discovered, it was too late to prevent the Confederates from capturing the Federals' guns.

While Federal leaders knew their troops were not ready for battle, they could not delay a move any longer. For weeks northern citizens had been crying for action. Twenty thousand rebels were now camped at Manassas, only thirty miles from Washington, near a winding little stream known as Bull Run. Why wait any longer, the Northerners wondered, to crush the upstart Confederates and shut down the new southern capital at Richmond, Virginia?

Although the troops were inexperienced, they were still splendid to watch as they marched out of Washington. The army was divided into three main branches—cavalry, artillery, and infantry. The cavalrymen looked the most impressive, high on their well-groomed horses, with curved sabers hanging at their sides. These were the soldiers who rode ahead in battle, serving as scouts or fast-moving raiders. The artillerymen on their way to Manassas also relied on horses, but they used these animals to haul heavy bronze cannon and ammunition wagons to the fighting zone. Riding aboard the wagons, the gunners stared straight ahead, grim and unsmiling. Soon they would be firing their heavy weapons and filling the air with scorching fire. When the cavalry and artillery had passed, the ranks of infantrymen still continued to come. These foot soldiers made up 80 percent of the fighting force in the Union Army.

The Federals cheered as they crossed the bridge leading into Virginia. Finally, they were entering the land where they would become heroes, where they would reunite the North and the South. But soon the troops grew quiet. The admiring crowds and the news reporters were far behind. The bands had stopped playing. Now there was only the fierce sun, the choking dust, and miles of marching ahead. The thick wool uniforms, which had once made the soldiers so proud, suddenly felt as heavy as armor. The men loosened their collars and unfastened their brass buttons. Some left their blanket rolls and knapsacks in the ditches beside the road. But there was no escaping the dust. The horses kicked the dried earth into a thick haze that settled in the soldiers' throats and noses.

After several hours of marching, the recruits forgot the lessons they had learned during drills on the parade ground. Exhausted and thirsty, some soldiers dropped out of line to gulp down water at a nearby creek. Others spotted blackberry bushes in the shade and without a second thought wandered off to fill their caps with the tempting fruit. The commander of this ragged army, General Irvin McDowell, was dismayed by his volunteers' lack of discipline. "They would not keep in the ranks," he later complained. "When they came where water was fresh they would pour the old water out of their canteens and fill them with fresh water; they were not used to denying themselves much."

By nightfall, many officers had completely lost patience with their men. Late in the day, the pace of the march had slowed to a shuffle. Every few minutes soldiers along the lines would come to a halt for no apparent reason. Abner Small, a volunteer from Maine, was a member of one slow-moving brigade. In his Civil War memoirs, Small described the maddening march to Bull Run. "We discovered the chief cause of the [halts] when we got to Accotink Run. Men of the brigade ahead of ours were crossing the creek in single file on a log." Soon the brigade commander rode up and found hundreds of men sitting on the bank and removing their shoes just in case they fell in the ankle-high water on their way across the unstable bridge. In disgust, the officer ordered his troops to trudge through the creek—shoes, socks, and all.

After two sluggish days of marching, the men were too tired and disorganized to charge straight into battle. They dragged into camps near Manassas to recover from the journey, while General McDowell investigated the area and created a battle plan. Just as the troops finished dinner on July 20, rumors of the general's attack plan began to sweep through the camps. They were marching into battle at dawn!

Although the soldiers had only a few hours to rest before they would have to shoulder their muskets, most could not sleep. Suddenly war had become more than a daydream. Many volunteers began to feel pangs of fear for the first time. A thoughtful silence settled over the camps as soldiers stared into their fires and wondered how they would feel when the first shots screamed by. Some men were more afraid of behaving like cowards than facing death. "I have a mortal dread of the battle field," wrote one private in a letter to his father. "I am afraid the groans of the wounded and dying will make me shake, nevertheless I hope & trust that strength will be given me to stand up & do my duty."

The advance into battle at Bull Run was nothing like the soldiers had expected. There was no glorious clash of armies on an open, level field. The troops were spread for miles among rolling hills, tangled woods, and marshy ravines. Without the training to perform a well-coordinated attack, each branch of the Army seemed to splinter off on a separate mission. The men in Abner Small's brigade encountered problems even before they reached the area of fighting. "We went on at the double-quick, but a mile of this

With its brambles and slippery shoreline, Bull Run presented a difficult obstacle for the soldiers who rushed into battle. Scores of men died along the banks of this meandering creek.

was all that we could do," Small revealed. "Men dropped, exhausted and fainting, by the wayside. . . . When we got to Bull Run at Sudley's Ford, many stopped to drink . . . drank too much; were lost to service for that day. Not half the brigade, nor half the regiment, crossed the run."

The cannon had already been roaring for several hours by the time Confederate Randolph McKim's unit reached the fighting zone. Hurrying closer to the rattle of gunfire, McKim was alarmed by what he saw behind the Confederate lines. Scores of wounded soldiers limped past him, their faces dazed with the look of sleepwalkers. Some men lay on stretchers, covered with blood and groaning in pain. Those who had less serious injuries called out to the fresh troops, describing how badly the fighting was going at the front. Even more startling, the commander of the rebel troops, General Joseph E. Johnston, had ordered McKim's brigade to "go where the fire is hottest."

Suddenly thrown into the thick of battle, the green recruits fought in wild confusion. Many were paralyzed for several awful seconds the first time they saw one of their officers or friends fall. As if events were happening in slow-motion, McKim noticed each detail of the lightening-like blast that struck down the leader of his brigade. Years later he still remembered exactly how the general had reeled in his saddle, thrown out his arms, and dropped to the ground. Several hundred yards away, across a wall of smoke and bullets, Abner Small was struggling through his own initiation into battle. "There was a wild uproar of shouting and firing," wrote Small. "The faces near me were inhuman. David Bates, one of my close comrades, was smashed by a solid shot; and what reply could we make to that? We wavered, and rallied, and fired blindly; and men fell writhing . . . we saw the glitter of bayonets coming against our flank; and we heard the order to retire. It was the turn of the tide."

As they retreated from the field, the Federal soldiers were stunned with fatigue and defeat. "Men near me were plodding heavily and panting," Small recalled. "Their faces were all sweat and grime, their eyes red from dust . . . . They were dirty and weary and angry. So was I. We made our way off the field as we would, without order or discipline."

The retreat soon turned into a panicked stampede. When the recruits reached the rear, they saw overturned supply wagons, abandoned equipment, and men rushing in all directions. Thinking that the Confederate cavalry must be ready to chase them down, the soldiers dropped their knapsacks and muskets, and broke into a run. To make matters worse, hundreds of sightseers from Washington clogged the army's roadway. Expecting to see a grand show

The Union troops were shaken and humiliated by the panic at Bull Run, portrayed in this illustration. As one soldier wrote to his family, "You will hear great stories about the bravery of this and that regiment of volunteers, but believe me, most of them acted like cowards in my division."

of military skill and courage, the spectators had come to Manassas with picnic hampers, tablecloths, and binoculars. Now congressmen in frockcoats and ladies in frilled dresses came running down from their picnic spots in terror. But their fancy carriages did not offer an easy escape. Although the drivers cracked their whips without mercy, the horses could not haul the coaches through the thick mud or the snarl of soldiers and sightseers.

The Federals later learned that there had been no reason to panic. At the end of the battle, the Confederates were just as disorganized as their defeated enemies. Instead of pursuing the Union Army, the southern recruits wandered about, looking for their regiments and surveying what was left on the battlefield. As they gazed over the blackened countryside, all they could see was acre after acre of dead soldiers and horses. Those who peered more closely at the corpses drew back in shock. "Some . . . seem to have had a terrible struggle with the monster death and only yielded after having suffered [horrible] pain," observed an Alabama private. "Their faces assume expressions that are fearful to look upon, their features distorted, the eyeballs glaring, and often with their hands full of mud and grass that they have clutched in their last agony." When McKim and several other men paused to drink from a stream, they realized that the water was tinged red with blood. Some were so thirsty that they drank from the brook anyway.

Slowly, the Confederates found their way back to camp. That night, as the rain dripped down, most were too exhausted to celebrate. By the light of the fire, they discussed the events of the day and wrote letters home about their grand victory. Before they sank into a heavy sleep, most could not help thinking of the dead soldiers who lay unburied in the rain. "As I lay down to sleep on the battlefield that night, I had much to think of," wrote McKim. "I had seen the reality of the battlefield . . . its awful pictures of the wounded, the dying, and the dead."

The next morning, however, the soldiers were ready to revel in their success by gathering up the treasures that the Yankees had left behind. The muskets, sabers, belt buckles, horses, and saddles would make fine trophies to show off back home.

The Federal soldiers did not have the delight of victory to

soften their grim first impressions of battle. They straggled back to Washington like lost sheep, suddenly realizing that this war would be no short and glorious affair. Soon the nation would learn the cost of Bull Run—3,000 Federals and 2,000 Confederates were dead, wounded or missing. But as Abner Small confessed, "I couldn't decide that numbers affected the first shock of seeing death in battle. One man or a thousand, the dead were dead."

Both citizens and soldiers in the North and South were shocked by the 5,000 casualties at the Battle of Bull Run. By the end of the war, however, these losses would seem light. During the Battle of Spotsylvania, when the Confederate shown above was killed, 12,000 men fell in one day on one square mile of ground.

Union soldiers relax on a hillside overlooking a camp veiled in smoke from cooking fires.

TWO

Campfires Burning

After the disaster at Manassas, the Federal soldiers were re-lieved to reach the safety of Washington. Only five days earlier they had itched to be off for war. Now they looked forward to the chance to lay down their muskets and sit quietly by the campfire. Some soldiers would soon put aside their weapons for good. Those who had enlisted for a period of three months were on their way home. They boarded trains back to their friends and families while the three-year volunteers looked on with envy.

That envy grew when the three-year recruits realized that the days of lazing in their tents and strolling through the city streets were over. A new leader had arrived to replace the unsuccessful General McDowell and take command of the newly christened Army of the Potomac. General George B. McClellan had promised President Lincoln that he could transform the gloomy and disorganized troops into a powerful army. He planned to begin this transformation in the camps. There, he insisted, the men would turn from ordinary citizens into soldiers. They would learn to move to the blare of trumpets and the beat of drums. They would learn to pitch a tent in minutes, jump to attention when officers passed, and march in darkness and driving rain. Most important, the thousands of soldiers from all shades of life would learn to act as one.

To begin his men's education, McClellan imposed strict new rules in camp. Recruits could no longer wander about Washington as they pleased. In order to leave camp, a soldier had to have a pass granted by his commanding officer. Military police swarmed through the saloons and gambling houses of the city, arresting all soldiers found away from their posts.

Once the recruits reported to camp, the officers immediately introduced them to a strenuous training schedule. Each morning a trumpet call roused the ranks at dawn. From daybreak until sundown, the men spent most of their time in the field, trying to absorb the basics of soldiering. While the drillmaster barked out orders, the volunteers struggled to keep their weapons up, bellies in, chests out, and heels in line. Overwhelmed by the flood of strange commands, the men often fumbled through the drills in complete confusion. "Drill is aching funny," wrote one recruit in his diary. "We are all green. Mistakes are corrected by making still worse mistakes. The men in the ranks grin, giggle and snicker, and now and then break out into a coarse country hee-haw."

To overcome these blunders, some officers held as many as five separate drill sessions each day. The tedious routine of marching exercises, bayonet practice, and rifle instruction seemed endless to many recruits. As one private from Pennsylvania described, "The first thing in the morning is drill. Then drill, then drill again. Then drill, drill, a little more drill. Then drill, and lastly drill."

During the brief periods when drill was dismissed, the soldiers had a full list of chores to keep them busy. General McClellan was fond of organization. He insisted that each camp function like a tidy city. The men set to work cleaning their tents, building pathways of pine logs, tending to horses, repairing equipment, and gathering firewood and water. There were also chores to guarantee that the enemy did not come too close. The soldiers took turns guarding the camp and helping with the construction of forts around Washington.

Many recruits were dismayed when they found themselves facing a daily routine of camp drudgery and drill. They had joined

Once the soldiers finally solved the mysteries of drilling with their 100-man companies, commanders held mass drills to teach recruits to maneuver within the larger units of regiments and brigades.

the army to fight, not dig ditches or obey the orders of picky officers. "A private soldier is nothing more than a slave and is often treated worse," complained one volunteer. To add to the soldiers' frustration, a large number of officers were just as ignorant about the rules of warfare as those they commanded. In the early days of war, it was common for volunteers to elect lower officers directly from the ranks of their military units. They usually chose the most popular man for company captain, instead of the man with the most intelligence or military experience. In a letter to his family about the unseasoned officers in camp, a soldier from Iowa commented, "It is rather a funny operation for one man to teach another what he don't know himself."

Of all the lessons taught during the war, obedience was the hardest for the strong-willed recruits to learn. If the soldiers disliked their officers, they frequently did not hesitate to tell them so. But McClellan was determined to teach discipline to his green troops. When a regiment from Maine refused to report for duty one morning, the general sent sixty-three of its members to prison for the remainder of the war. How could soldiers be expected to follow orders on the battlefield, McClellan asked his commanders, if they could not obey orders in camp?

The officers relied on a strange variety of punishments to hammer discipline into their troops. Private Alfred Bellard from New Jersey was among the first soldiers in the Army of the Potomac to become familiar with these methods. Bellard, along with thousands of other Union volunteers, arrived in Washington in August to replace the departing three-month recruits. Before long, the commander of Bellard's regiment was holding his first inspection, checking carefully to make sure each soldier had combed his hair, washed his uniform, and cleaned his gun. While Bellard was excused from guard duty for cleanliness, several men in his company were punished for not polishing their shoes. "Each of them were provided with a [log] instead of a gun, and had to parade in front of the guard tent for the rest of the day," Bellard described in his Civil War memoirs. Not only did the men feel ridiculous for marching with logs on their shoulders, but they also grew weary as the hours wore on. Small logs that felt light in the morning seemed as heavy as tree trunks by the end of the day.

Like log carrying, most punishments were designed to humiliate soldiers. For minor offenses such as drinking liquor or leaving camp without permission, recruits were often sentenced to wear the "barrel shirt." The offender would waddle around camp in a large wooden barrel, with his arms sticking through holes cut in the sides and his head poking from a hole in the top. For more serious offenses such as speaking disrespectfully to superiors, the officers in Bellard's regiment had a favorite penalty known as "bucking and gagging." The soldiers dreaded this punishment, for it was painful as well as degrading. Gagged with a stick tied in his mouth, the culprit was seated on the ground with his hands tied together in front of him. Then his knees were forced between his elbows and another stick was shoved between his arms and knees. As Bellard described, the unfortunate victim was pinned like a trapped rat in a horribly cramped position.

Despite the strict schedules and sometimes cruel punishments,

Punishments varied from one regiment to the next. This soldier, who stole from a wounded friend, was sentenced to have his head shaved and wear a large sign labeling him as a thief. To add to his shame, the culprit was forced out of camp, marching to the music of a fife and drum.

the men in the Army of the Potomac thrived during the fall of 1861. Under General McClellan's untiring rule, they ate hearty food, slept in clean quarters, and for the first time felt like true soldiers. The recruits had begun to feel pride in their newfound discipline. This pride reached its peak when McClellan held a grand review of his troops in November.

On a raw, wintry day, the entire army—eighty thousand strong—assembled in a broad field several miles from the Capitol. As the dashing young general on his huge horse galloped past the countless rows of men, a wild cheer swept through the ranks. Then the soldiers stood at attention for more than two hours while McClellan escorted President Lincoln up and down the lines. Afterwards the two leaders climbed the reviewing stand to watch the vast army march by in perfect step. A colonel from Pennsylvania later described the spectacular scene: "The ground trembled under the steady tread of the endless columns of disciplined soldiers. . . . In the realization of all observers, even the most experienced officers, the army was born that day."

Thirty miles away, on the other side of the Potomac River, the Confederate troops waited for the grand Union Army to spring into action. After their triumph at Bull Run, General Johnston and the other Confederate commanders decided to allow the Yankees to make the next move. But McClellan, who was determined to avoid another Union failure, would not be ready to move until spring. As the colder months approached, an uneasy calm settled over the southern camps around Manassas. Satisfied that the fighting was finished for the year, the Confederate officers gave their men permission to "go into winter quarters."

After weeks of sleeping in tents and lying on the hard ground, the soldiers excitedly set about building more permanent homes. With axes over their shoulders, they spread out in all directions to chop logs for their huts, leaving acres of stumps behind them. Usually four men worked together to build a shelter. They shared the tedious work of notching and laying the logs, then filling the cracks with wood chips and mud. Finally came the roof, which was made from boards, shingles, or often a simple tent cloth.

The soldiers entertained themselves putting the final touches on their rustic cabins, a welcome break from battlefield duty and

Wood often grew scarce when the troops moved into winter quarters. The soldiers needed wood not only to build their shelters, but also for cooking food, heating huts, and constructing walkways across the muddy clearings.

drill. The men delighted in using their imaginations to provide furnishings for their new homes. For candlestick holders, they used their bayonets driven into the ground. Stumps or shipping crates became stools. Ammunition chests became tables. They built bunks, padding them with pine needles, straw, or leaves. They made fireplaces of sticks daubed with mud, adding a barrel for a chimney. For the crowning touch, the soldiers gave names to their homes, such as "Buzzard's Roost," "Swine Hotel," "Hole in the Wall," "Devil's Inn," and "The House That Jack Built."

Although most of these shelters were no more than shacks, the men took great pride in their makeshift homes. One Texan who was camped in Virginia happily boasted in a letter to his mother, "We have finished our house. . . . We have the best fire place and chimney in the company. . . . our guns are in racks on the walls; our utensils consist of one skillet, a stew kettle, a bread pan, a fying pan, & a large kettle." Another Confederate wrote, "We'll soon have quite a 'log cabin' city, and one that will take a larger force of Yankees to make us desert."

After they had settled into winter quarters, many officers invited their wives to visit. The owners of this sturdy cabin had the rare comfort of a brick fireplace topped with a barrel to direct the smoke.

Many soldiers took time to attend religious services held by regimental chaplains. "The gathering each night of bronzed and grizzly warriors devoutly worshipping was a wonderful picture in the army," wrote a Virginia volunteer. Unfortunately, there were never enough chaplains to serve either side.

For the soldiers, winter quarters not only meant more comfortable housing, it also meant more free time. Snow and ice often made drills impossible. And with the Union Army tucked away in its own winter camps, the Confederate officers felt more inclined to give the men time to do as they pleased. The soldiers had no trouble inventing ways to escape the sometimes dull routine of camp life. After the hard work of earlier months, they appreciated even the simplest pastimes. Describing the favorite amusements of the soldiers in his cabin, one southern recruit in General Johnston's army wrote, "[We] had a few books, a set of chess men, took one daily paper and kept on hand a supply of writing materials. [We] became experts in making loaf bread and telling yarns."

Of all the soldiers' pastimes, letter writing was the favorite. While Union mail wagons were nearly always full, the shortage of writing materials in the South prevented Confederates from corresponding as often. To solve this problem, some men made ink from the juice of pokeberries or reused old letters, writing between the lines.

One of the most popular forms of entertainment in both armies was music. The soldiers had left for war with bands blaring and crowds singing patriotic songs. On the march they bellowed battle hymns. On guard duty they whistled softly to themselves as they paced back and forth. And on peaceful nights, small groups of soldiers gathered around the campfires to sing. The favorite tunes were sentimental ballads—"Home Sweet Home," "Just Before the Battle, Mother," "The Girl I Left Behind Me," "When This Cruel War Is Over"—songs that gave the soldiers a chance to reveal freely their feelings of fear or homesickness.

Sometimes the men joined together to stage more formal mu-

"Just Before the Battle, Mother" was one of the most popular ballads written during the Civil War. Gathered around the campfire, some soldiers had to brush away tears as they sang the refrain, "Farewell mother, you may never press me to your heart again."

sical activities. In the Fourth Texas Regiment, which was camped near the Potomac River in 1861, a group of soldiers formed a company of players. They called themselves "Hood's Minstrels" in honor of their commander, General John Bell Hood. Before long the troop had also organized a brass band, a choir of singers, and a team of soldiers to help build a theater. One artistic recruit volunteered to decorate the curtain for the stage. Made from an old tent cloth, the curtain itself was enough to attract audiences. On it, the soldier painted a strange scene of devils and sea monsters with fierce green eyes and lolling tongues. The theater opened to large crowds of soldiers and continued to be packed for every performance. Although most of the men were constantly short of money, they gladly paid twenty-five cents to see the show.

Many soldiers also spent their precious pay on pastimes that were not quite so innocent. Away from the restraints of home for the first time, some recruits responded to their new freedom by acting wild. One young Virginian who was shocked by his fellow soldiers' off-duty behavior wrote, "There is some of the most [ornery] men here that I ever saw and the most swearing and card playing and [fighting] and drunkenness that I ever saw at any place." Like the camps under McClellan's command, the Confederate Army imposed strict rules against drinking liquor and gambling. But as the war dragged on, most officers gave up trying to enforce the restrictions on gambling. Betting was a passion among the soldiers. They would risk their money on anything: cards, dice games, cockfights, wrestling matches, baseball, and raffles. Men in the First Tennessee Regiment even held races between lice on tin plates, placing bets on which insect could crawl the fastest.

Socializing with the enemy was another forbidden activity that was common throughout the war. During the lull between battles, the opposing sides often posted guards known as pickets within shouting distance of one another. The majority of these soldiers could not resist the temptation to call out to the mysterious foe who stood only yards away. Frequently, the enemies exchanged insults and curses. But just as often, the conversations were surprisingly friendly. The soldiers even traded small luxuries. "Although intercourse with the enemy was strictly forbidden," revealed a recruit, "the men were on the most friendly terms . . . conversing

Beneath the shade of pine boughs covering a campsite near Petersburg, Virginia, a Federal general and his staff wait for servants to release fighting cocks. In this gruesome sport, soldiers bet money on which rooster could overcome the other with its beak and claws.

and exchanging such commodities as coffee, sugar, tobacco, corn meal and newspapers." If rivers and lakes separated the enemy lines, the soldiers loaded their treasures on little hand-carved sailboats and sent them bobbing across to the men who waited on the far shore.

Whenever soldiers from the North and South did manage to hold a serious conversation, they were strangely moved by how much they had in common. They often shared the same backgrounds, the same likes and dislikes, the same fears. Their respect for one another often outweighed their resentments. One Confederate soldier, after a long talk with a Union man, wrote home sadly, "We could have settled the war in 30 minutes had it been left to us."

As the weeks in winter camp stretched into months, the novelty of the soldiers' pastimes began to fade. Both armies would spend seven months in camp before their leaders ordered them on to the next battle in March 1862. Meanwhile, the men began to feel like caged animals. In January, Private Robert Moore of the Seventeenth Mississippi Regiment complained in his diary: "The weather still continues disagreeable. . . . Every person seems drowsy in camp. No amusements in camp. . . . All are becoming tired of such inactive life, but we will be doomed to remain here for some time to come." A rash of fighting and quarreling broke out among the ranks during these gloomy days. Log huts that had once seemed cozy now felt crowded and stifling. Bunkmates who had once made the others laugh with their jokes and pranks now seemed obnoxious and annoying.

Army food was one of the main reasons for discontent among the men. In the first days of war, rations were fairly plentiful. But it was not long before shortages began to occur. As early as July 1861, soldiers on the southern side began to go hungry. A commander at Manassas asked Confederate President Jefferson Davis not to send more troops to the front because, as he wrote, "Some regiments are nearly starving." Both armies suffered on the march. During battle campaigns, the men often moved faster than their supply wagons or camped far away from food-producing areas. Private Oliver Norton wrote to his sister, "I have marched forty-six miles on nothing but raw beef and ditch water, and yet I held out to the end."

When the soldiers did receive rations, the food ranged from tasteless to disgusting. A large amount of food rotted by the time it reached the troops. To keep beef and pork from going bad, the army frequently pickled the meat in a briny saltwater solution. This process made the beef so salty that the soldiers usually soaked the foul-smelling pieces in water for several hours before attempting to eat them. The soldiers' cooking methods did not improve matters. The men prepared the so-called "salt-horse" by frying it in globs of grease, which caused countless stomach problems among the ranks. One doctor in the Union Army reported that he was having trouble preventing "death from the frying pan."

Fresh vegetables were even scarcer than fresh beef. As a substitute, the government issued a strange concoction called "desiccated vegetables." This assortment supposedly consisted of beans, onions, turnips, carrots, and beets—all dried and pressed into hard, bland cakes. But when the soldiers inspected the cakes more closely, they also found roots, stalks, and leaves, and so began to call the mixture "baled hay." The men tried to disguise the desiccated vegetables in soup—usually unsuccessfully. After adding water to the cakes, one officer was reminded of a "dirty brook with all the dead leaves floating around."

With the lack of fresh food, the Federals resorted to satisfying their hunger on flour-and-water crackers called "hardtack." These biscuits were a half-inch thick and so hard that they earned nicknames such as "teeth dullers" and "sheet-iron crackers." Even worse, the hardtack was frequently infested with worms and weevils. One soldier counted thirty-two worms in a single cracker. The hungry men, however, were amazingly tolerant of the creatures in their food. As another volunteer described, "It was no uncommon occurrence for a man to find the surface of his pot of coffee swimming with weevils after breaking hardtack in it . . . but they were easily skimmed off and left no distinctive flavor behind."

For bread rations, the Confederates received corn bread more often than hardtack. But according to their reports, this was no better. "The corn bread would get so hard and moldy that when we broke it, it looked like it had cobwebs in it," a Southerner recalled.

Poor rations and other hardships of army life took their toll on the soldiers. As the two sides sank deeper into war, the clean-swept camps and healthy ranks that McClellan had dreamed of became harder and harder to find. Sickness from malnourishment plagued thousands of soldiers. Disease from unsanitary conditions struck down thousands more. During long periods of rain and snow, the camp streets were churned into rivers of mud. The log huts sprang leaks and wind whistled through the cracks. But soon the passing of winter signaled the return to battle. For those who had survived the discipline, boredom, and revolting food of camp days, the true test of spirit was yet to come.

With its gun carriages, heavy cannon, horse teams, and loads of ammunition, the artillery was the most time-consuming branch of the army to assemble before battle.

THREE

Newcomers No More

In July 1862, Private Oliver Norton received a letter from his sister asking him to describe his feelings during battle. Norton, a member of the Army of the Potomac, had just scraped through the bloody Seven Days' battles during McClellan's march toward the Confederate capital of Richmond. The frantic scenes of fighting were still sharp in his mind. He wrote back to his sister quickly, vividly describing the rage that seized him when he watched his colonel and two best friends fall. "I was stronger than I had been before in a month," Norton scribbled. "Scenes that would have unnerved me at other times had no effect."

Bullets whizzed past, the Pennsylvanian told his sister. But the closer they flew, the more fearless he became. One bullet knocked his rifle to splinters. Norton simply snatched a gun from a man nearby who had staggered to the ground, shot through the head. He jumped over dead bodies as if they were boulders in the road, thinking only of how he could kill as many rebels as possible.

Norton was amazed by his own burst of courage; but such bravery was not unusual among soldiers under fire. As the volunteers marched from one bloody battlefield to another, the panic that had paralyzed the troops at Bull Run became less common.

The men no longer felt like farmers, lawyers, students, and store-keepers in uniform. They were now specialists in the business of war.

Officers filled Civil War record books with accounts of their soldiers' shining deeds. Again and again volunteers rushed forward in battle when they knew it was nearly impossible to survive. They charged up hills under deadly hailstorms of bullets. They risked their own lives to pull injured comrades away from the line of fire. Even after being horribly wounded, flagbearers struggled to hold the banners of their regiments high. One Confederate officer reported that his men fought gallantly in spite of the fact that many did not have shoes to wear. The soldiers ran through thorns and briars without pausing, some leaving bloody footprints along the way.

But while many soldiers continued to perform like bold heroes in the field, most never completely lost their fear of combat. "For myself, I must confess that the terrors of the battlefield grew not less as we advanced in the war," wrote twenty-year-old Confederate John Dooley in his journal. "In every battle [soldiers] see so many new forms of death . . . that their dread of [suffering such] fearful perils unnerves them for each succeeding conflict."

The hours approaching battle were often more nerve-wracking than the fighting itself. Preparations were slow and suspenseful. It sometimes took days, even weeks, for the soldiers to move from winter quarters to the fighting zone. Once the troops had assembled, three days of rations were issued to hold the men through long stretches of battle. Next, ammunition was dispensed; weapons were inspected; officers gave rousing speeches and final instructions. By the time the steady roll of drums signaled the army to advance, the suspense had often become unbearable.

For many soldiers, the waiting continued. Some units were marched to their assigned positions and commanded to halt until further orders. Frequently hours passed before more orders arrived. "Half an hour upon an occasion like this seems an age," described a young captain from Texas. "The feelings that take possession of a soldier on the eve of advancing into a fight can be known only to those who have experienced them. The heart is heavy; the blood feels as if it was congealed; the breath comes short and quick, and it is a relief to move on."

Some men tried to cover or ease their tension by acting as if they were spending an ordinary day in camp. They tried to joke and talk, but their conversations and laughter sounded stiff and insincere. On their way into the bloody Battle of Gettysburg, John Dooley's regiment passed by gravediggers who were busy burying the mangled corpses from the previous day of fighting. A few minutes later Dooley and his fellow soldiers were nervously pelting each other with green apples that lay in the hollow where they waited to charge.

As the moment to attack drew closer, the troops fell quiet. Thousands of comrades crouched together along the edge of the battlefield. Yet most of the soldiers felt entirely alone. Just before battle, many men fought a private war with their emotions. They prayed, promising God they would never sin again if He would carry them through the fight unharmed. They thought longingly of their families and homes. Scattered among the ranks were soldiers who felt an eerie sense of dread, convinced that they would not live through another day. Some wrote their names on small slips of paper, which they pinned to their uniforms so they could be identified in case they were killed in action. Others turned their belongings over to close friends with instructions on where to send them after they died.

The blast of cannon often jolted the soldiers out of their quiet reflections. In the Battle of Gettysburg, Dooley and the men of the First Virginia received orders to lie down while their artillery opened fire on the enemy. According to instructions, the 150 Confederate cannon would cease firing after one hour, signaling the soldiers to charge across the open field and "sweep from [their] path anything in the shape of a Yankee." As the men lay with their faces pressed to the dry grass, their hearts seemed to thump the ground. The Union forces returned fire. With each second, the missiles mowed down more and more men. In one regiment positioned near Dooley's, eighty-eight rebels were killed before the charge even began. "Around, above, beneath, and on all sides [the shells] schreech, sing, scream, whistle, roar, whirr, buzz, bang, and whizz," Dooley described. "And we are obliged to lie quietly tho' frightened out of our wits. . . ."

Finally, the order to advance ended this agonizing suspense.

During Civil War times, gunners had to identify their targets with their own eyes and use their best judgment to hit their mark. Here, officers of the 55th New York pose with a huge cannon at Fort Gaines, a major fortification protecting Washington, D.C.

But the rush of relief from waiting did not last long. The men rose to their feet, marched a few steps, and found themselves in a storm of crashing shells. When the smoke cleared for an instant, the troops could see the unbroken line of enemy soldiers in the distance, stiffening for the assault. The line bristled with dark

muskets and flashing bayonets. Battle flags flapped in the breeze.

In these moments the months of drills began to make sense. To launch a successful attack, the soldiers had to perform a series of movements in unison. They were expected to move forward steadily, elbow to elbow, keeping a distance of thirteen inches from the soldier in front. The fighting line might have to shift to the right or left, or quickly close up a gap left by the deadly cannonfire. As the Virginians at Gettysburg pressed ahead, their officers shouted out a string of commands: "Steady—dress to the right—give way to the left—keep well in line . . . ." But the rebels could barely hear the hoarse commands above the thundering gunfire. In the midst of the uproar, the captain of John Dooley's company was suddenly shot down. The troops were left without a leader, until Dooley himself rushed forward to take the captain's place.

As the soldiers moved within firing range of the enemy, they also began to appreciate the tedious weaponry drills from their days in camp. Firing a musket in battle was an awkward and difficult process. Each reload involved nine separate steps. One step required the soldiers to use their teeth to break open a cartridge containing a bullet and gunpowder. The men would emerge from each battle looking like ghouls, their lips black from biting into powder cartridges.

In the chaos of fighting, some soldiers failed to complete all of the loading steps they had learned in drill. After pouring powder down the barrel of the gun and inserting a bullet, the men remembered to tamp down the cartridge with a ramrod. But once in a while they forgot to remove the rods from their gun barrels. When they pulled the trigger, the rods sailed into the air like spears. Other soldiers spent the battle using rifles that, for one reason or another, never fired. They rammed load after load down their rifle barrels without realizing that their efforts produced no results. After the Battle of Gettysburg, the victors found thousands of rifles on the field that held more than one load.

With the frantic firing of muskets and enemy shells ripping through their ranks, most attacking soldiers eventually became disorganized. If a man wanted to run from action, he usually chose one of these moments for his escape. The smoke and confusion gave panicky soldiers a perfect chance to slip away unnoticed. Deserters who were caught in the act often had to endure teasing and insults from the other men. But most preferred this treatment to the abuse they received from furious officers. During a brutal round of cannonfire, one frightened soldier made a ridiculous sight as he tried to shelter himself by hiding behind a flimsy cracker box. A colonel who spotted the man crouching behind the crate strode up and kicked him out of his hiding place, saying, "You will disgrace my regiment." Other commanders were even harsher in their treatment of cowards. Some appointed soldiers to march in the rear of the ranks during battle and shoot down anyone who tried to run away.

As the advance continued, officers called a halt to reassemble their scattered men and prepare for the final dash toward the opposing lines. At this point commanders also gave the order to "fix bayonets," and the soldiers quickly fitted long steel blades over the ends of their musket barrels. Then came the order to "charge,"

Each officer shown in this photograph was wounded at the Battle of Gettysburg. Francis C. Barlow (at left), the "boy-general" leaning his back against the tree, almost died from his injuries.

and the troops surged forward with a cheer. As the First Virginia soldiers ran the last few yards of their nightmarish attack at Gettysburg, Dooley was shot through both thighs. He fell to the ground, but could still hear his fellow soldiers raise the wild, piercing "rebel yell" when they threw themselves against the Union forces.

Hand-to-hand combat in the Civil War was uncontrolled and vicious. The soldiers fired at such close range that the blast from their muskets scorched their victims. However, the men could usually fire no more than one shot when fighting face to face. There was not enough time to reload, so the desperate soldiers used whatever method they could find to survive. They jabbed with their bayonets or swung their rifles like clubs. Those who lost their guns in the confusion pounded their enemies with stones, fence rails, or fists. One survivor described the fighting at Gettysburg: "Foot to foot, body to body and man to man they struggled, pushed, and strived and killed. Each had rather die than yield."

For those in the midst of such confusion, it was often difficult to tell which side was winning. The soldiers fought furiously, concentrating on the dangers directly in front of them. Most never had a chance to look around and observe the overall situation. When John Dooley fell only thirty yards from the line of Union guns, he still had no idea how the Confederate charge would end. As he lay on the field listening to the last minutes of fighting, he was tortured more by his curiosity than his wounds. But soon Dooley heard the Yankees raise their own victorious cry—a deep-voiced, roaring hurrah. With a feeling of horror, he realized that the attack had failed.

Each battle had a new effect on the soldiers' attitudes toward war. Bull Run and the clashes of 1862 had forced men to realize the tragic truth: War was ugly and heartbreaking. But until Gettysburg, no one had fully realized how destructive war could be. Gettysburg was the biggest battle ever fought in American history. In three days of fighting, the Union lost 23,000 men, and the Confederacy even more. Soldiers and citizens everywhere began to wonder whether victory could be worth such a terrible price.

But while they were shocked by the losses of Gettysburg, many veterans found that with each battle they were becoming less and less appalled by the grim scenes of suffering. Men who had once turned away from corpses in horror and disgust could now sleep next to a dead body without losing a minute of rest. Some were distressed by this hardening process. "I can look at a dead man or help a wounded man from the field and think no more of it than I would of eating my dinner," Private Henry Schafer confessed to his family. "I am ashamed to say it but I have seen so much

Across the countryside, barren cemeteries marked the scenes of battles. Sadly, many of the graves were nameless, without markers or tombstones.

of it that . . . I have become hardened and it does not affect me but little to walk over the field of strife and behold its horrors."

Some soldiers even began to joke about their dead comrades. When an Illinois regiment passed through a battlefield a month after the fighting, they spotted the hand of a corpse sticking up through the dirt on a shallow grave. One disrespectful soldier placed a hardtack biscuit in the hand, while another called out from the ranks, "That fellow was not going off hungry if he could help it!"

Along with their sensitivity, a large number of soldiers also began to lose their willingness to fight. In the early days of war, men were disgraced by the thought of shirking their duties and sneaking back home. But by the winter of 1862, desertion had become a common crime in both armies. Defeat had a devastating effect on the morale of the volunteers. After the failure at Gettysburg, dozens of southern soldiers decided that the Confederate efforts were hopeless. They left their posts, thinking that it would be senseless to continue risking their lives for a lost cause. Other soldiers lost patience with the hardships of army life—the poor rations, harsh winters, and diseased camps. "If I ever lose my patriotism," one private wrote home, ". . . then you may know the 'Commissary' is at fault. Corn meal mixed with water and tough beef three times a day will knock the 'Brave Volunteer' under quicker than Yankee bullets."

While many soldiers could tolerate their own difficulties, they could not bear to remain in the army knowing that their families suffered while they were away. Letters from wives and relatives frequently brought bad news of sickness, failing crops, or lack of food and money. Since most of the war was fought on Confederate territory, southern soldiers had more reasons to worry about their families. During their march through the South, the invading troops swept over some towns like a plague of locusts. They scoured an area for food, often burning homes and robbing valuable property before moving on. With this threat to their loved ones, countless soldiers could not resist the urge to desert just to protect their homes.

Some volunteers resorted to drastic measures to be released from the army. A Confederate from Louisiana wished for a mild battle wound so that he could receive several weeks of leave to recover at home. If "some friendly bullet" would "hit me just severely enough to send me home for 60 or 90 days," he wrote to his mother, "I would gladly welcome such a bullet and consider the Yankee who fired it as a good kind fellow." A surprising number of desperate soldiers who passed through battle without a wound decided to take care of the job themselves. While on guard duty, one Union soldier shot off three of his fingers by pushing the trigger of his musket with a stick.

Deserters who were caught never knew what penalty to expect. In the beginning of the war, when the ranks were full, punishments for desertion were fairly light. An offender might have to spend two months in the guardhouse, clean stables for two weeks, or drag a heavy ball and chain from his ankle for ten days. But soon a lack of manpower in the armies became an urgent problem. As the number of deserters reached the tens of thousands, punishments grew harsher. One unlucky private was given fifty lashes on his bare back, then had the left side of his head shaved. But that was not all. After the letter "D" for deserter was branded on the culprit's left hip with a red-hot iron, he was forced to wear a ball and chain for six months. As a final humiliation, the private was drummed out of service to the jaunty tune of the "Rogue's March" while his fellow soldiers looked on.

In rare cases, the military courts decided to set a severe example by imposing the harshest sentence of all: death. Those who witnessed the killing of deserters were often haunted by the disturbing memory for years. The executions were slow and ceremonious. Once the troops had lined up to watch the event, the condemned man was marched onto an open field. Sometimes a group of soldiers led the way, carrying an empty coffin. After the prisoner had joined the chaplain in prayer, he was usually blindfolded and seated on the coffin's edge. Then amid an awful stillness, a squad of soldiers raised their rifles and fired. "It was hard to bear," wrote one Federal spectator. "Faces paled and hands shook which were not accustomed to show fear."

Sometimes the members of a firing squad made the scene more horrible by missing their target. In an execution of two Confederate deserters, the squad succeeded in killing one prisoner, but only

Standing behind his own coffin, a deserter awaits execution while members of the firing squad bow their heads for the chaplain's final prayer. In the background, members of the condemned man's regiment line up to watch the ceremony.

wounded the other. As the dying man groaned, "Lord, have mercy on me," the officer in charge ordered four more soldiers to step within two paces of the prisoner and fire again. Fortunately, their bullets ended the man's misery.

Although such punishments for desertion were frightening, nothing could hold back the flood of soldiers who wanted to escape from the army. To make matters worse, fewer and fewer men stepped forward to fill the vacant spots left by deserters and those killed in battle. Searching for ways to maintain their armies, both sides adopted draft laws that forced young, healthy men to enlist. But while the draft increased manpower, it also caused the quality of regiments to drop. The units were corrupted by men who detested what they were doing. They sulked and dragged through their duties, and in the end, often caused more problems than they were worth.

The Union Army also tried to attract more men by offering a bonus of one hundred dollars to all volunteers. As the war continued, states and cities paid additional cash for enlistments. By

1864, a man could make large sums of money before he had ever served any time. Like the draft laws, this bounty system brought in many recruits who offered little help. Men who had no desire to become soldiers would join the army, collect the money, desert, then collect another bonus by enlisting again under a different name.

This cartoon ridicules the southern recruiting system. Faced with a drop in the number of volunteers, the Confederacy adopted draft laws in 1862—eleven months earlier than the Union. As this drawing illustrates, men who were forced into the army by law were a distinct cut below those who enlisted out of patriotism.

These outlaws not only made trouble, but they also caused the morale in the regiments to sag. Veterans despised these so-called bounty jumpers. Members of the Thirteenth Massachusetts sank into depression when 186 bounty jumpers, drafted soldiers, and other rough-looking characters arrived supposedly to reinforce the regiment. "Strong men, particularly soldiers, are not easily moved to tears," wrote a veteran, "yet the cheeks of a good many men were wet as they gazed on these ruffians. . . . The pride which we felt in the membership of the Thirteenth turned to bitterness at sight of these fellows."

For every deserter or bounty jumper, there were several soldiers who were determined to stand by their posts until the end of the war. Most of these men did not suffer through the hardships of war quietly. Even after months of service, veterans still complained about long marches, foolish leaders, and late pay. But while they grumbled endlessly about living conditions, they accepted their duty to fight without complaint. As one Federal soldier vowed in 1863, "I am determined to do my duty and come home honorably or never."

Some volunteers maintained this sense of honor until their last breath. Private J. R. Montgomery, a Confederate who was mortally wounded in 1864, gracefully accepted death as a natural part of a soldier's life. On paper stained with spots of blood from his wound, Montgomery wrote this note to his father in Mississippi:

> Dear Father,
> This is my last letter to you. . . . I have been struck by a piece of shell and my right shoulder is horribly mangled and I know death is inevitable. . . . I know death is near, that I will die far from home and friends of my early youth, but I have friends here too who are kind to me. My friend Fairfax will write you at my request and give you the particulars of my death. My grave will be marked 58 that you may visit if you desire to do so. . . . Give my love to all my friends . . . my strength fails me. . . . May we meet in heaven.
> Your dying son,
> J. R. Montgomery

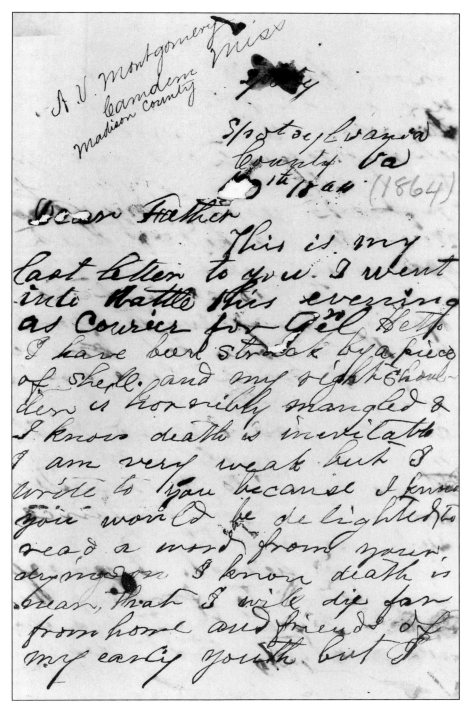

Private J. R. Montgomery's last letter to his father, stained with spots of blood from his battle wound.

Workers at Andersonville bury the victims of starvation and disease in a shallow mass grave. In one day in 1864, the death toll at the camp reached 127—or one death every eleven minutes.

FOUR

Patients and Prisoners

"**O**h what stories I shall have to tell you one of these days," a young woman named Katharine Wormeley wrote to her mother in 1862. For three months Wormeley worked as a nurse aboard steamboats that sailed up and down the East Coast, carrying wounded Federal soldiers from battlefields to hospitals. Most of her stories about life on these floating clinics were heartbreaking. After each battle, bleeding men filled the decks, stairs, and passageways of the relief boats. Stretcher after stretcher arrived until there was barely enough room for the nurses to step as they picked their way through the bodies, passing out brandy and bread.

When the steamers were not crowded with the wounded, they were filled with the sick. As Wormeley observed, "It is not a battle which destroys so many lives as it is the terrible . . . diseases brought on by exposure and hardships." By the time they were laid upon the decks, some soldiers were so weak with fever and hunger that they were completely helpless. The nurses set to work feeding these patients, one by one, spoonful by spoonful. Then they brought buckets of soap and water to wash away weeks of filth. As Katharine Wormeley set about this chore, she frequently emptied her dirty water and replaced it with fresh. But one old soldier stopped her. "Stop, marm!" he cried. "That water will do for several of us yet. Bless you! I make my coffee of worse than that."

Like others, this soldier had no idea that drinking dirty water was probably the exact reason for his illness. Even most doctors during the Civil War did not know what caused the diseases that plagued thousands of soldiers. This lack of medical knowledge had deadly effects. In the Union Army, four men died of sickness for every one killed in battle. In the Confederate Army, death from disease was even more common.

Both sides were totally unprepared to take care of the ever-growing number of sick soldiers. Medical efforts were hindered not only by scientific ignorance, but by a severe shortage of hospitals, doctors, and supplies. At the beginning of the war, the U.S. Medical Department owned just twenty thermometers and no more than six stethoscopes. Neither side had guessed that their worst enemy would be invisible. Now the armies had bitter lessons to learn in the war against mysterious germs.

The army medical departments made their first mistakes before the earliest volunteers had even been sworn into the service. To enlist, each man had to pass a physical examination. There were strict guidelines for inspecting recruits. But in their eagerness to sign up as many soldiers as possible, officials often ignored the rules and approved unhealthy men for duty. Some physicians gave medical exams so quickly that the soldiers never realized they were being examined. A surgeon in Chicago approved an entire regiment after having the 1,000 men trot past him in the rain. Other doctors were a bit more thorough. As one volunteer described the inspection his regiment received, "[The doctor] would give us a thump on the chest, and if we were not floored nor showed any other signs of inconvenience, we were pronounced in good condition. . . . "

Once the soldiers had passed their medical exams and made it to camp, they often found that the size of their regiments dropped drastically within the first few months. The rough living conditions quickly weeded out those who were too old, too young, or too sickly for service. But army life also struck down strong, hardy recruits—even in camps that were clean and well-stocked. A large number of soldiers were farmers who came from isolated areas and had never been exposed to diseases such as measles, mumps, or chicken pox. In the crowded living quarters of camp, contagious illnesses spread rapidly. Men who had been healthy their whole lives dropped like a line of falling dominoes.

No sooner had soldiers recovered from their first bout of illness than they were struck down by a new round of more deadly infections—diseases that lived in the filth of the camps. In the unsettled days of war, most recruits did not give much thought to cleanliness. Although army regulations recommended baths every three or four days, some men went for weeks without washing themselves or their clothing. Under the command of lenient officers, camps grew just as dirty as the soldiers. The troops left garbage and heaps of animal manure along the pathways. They dug latrines within steps of their living quarters. On the march, the men often pitched their tents near stagnant swamps where millions of disease-carrying mosquitoes swarmed.

Along with mosquitoes, hordes of lice and fleas infested the slovenly camps. When soldiers first discovered these insects creeping over their bodies, they were ashamed and disgusted. Some men crept away to scrub themselves in nearby streams or frantically shake out their clothing. But soon each soldier realized that his tentmates were also scratching more than usual. It became clear that the pests were everywhere—and inescapable. "There is not a man in the army, officer or private, that does not have from a Batallion to a Brigade of Body lice on him," concluded a soldier from Alabama. "I could soon get rid of them," he went on, "but there is always some filthy man in camps that [perpetuates] the race."

Although the soldiers could not identify the exact causes of their ailments, they gradually learned that there was a definite link between dirt and disease. In the last two years of the war, sanitation improved. But not before thousands of men drank contaminated water and died from typhoid fever. Thousands more were bitten by infected mosquitoes and stricken with malaria. Of all wartime diseases, the most common was dysentery, an intestinal disorder causing severe diarrhea. In 1862, the Army of the Potomac reported that 995 out of every 1,000 men suffered from diarrhea and dysentery. While these ailments were far less fatal than some of the other conditions, they left victims weak and susceptible to more serious illnesses.

Naturally, many soldiers began to believe that the battle against disease was hopeless. John Haley, a volunteer from Maine, scribbled angrily in his journal, "Short rations, bog water to drink, malaria inhaled with every breath, homesickness, and added to all this an incompetent surgeon. Is it any wonder that we are being swept off at the rate of two per day?"

Haley's criticism of his regiment's surgeon was typical. With more and more friends dying every day, the soldiers could not help but search for someone to blame. Doctors were a natural target. In many cases, however, there were good reasons for the soldiers to question their doctors' abilities. Some surgeons had learned their trade merely by watching practicing physicians at work. The majority of Civil War surgeons had earned a medical degree, but this achievement did not necessarily represent a long or challenging period of training. To qualify for medical school, an applicant needed only to be the proper age and be able to pay the tuition. Schooling lasted only two years, and the second year of study was nothing more than a repeat of the first.

Doctors graduated from this brief training program knowing very little about the treatment of disease. What they did learn from their instructors was often completely wrong. For example, some physicians believed that they could "draw out" sickness by making their patients sweat or bleed. To treat pneumonia, they rubbed burning alcohol on a sick soldier's chest, applied hot bricks to his feet, or even cut his wrists. For stomach complaints, doctors frequently recommended that their patients wear flannel body bandages or strange inventions known as stomach belts.

The medicines that many doctors prescribed were not much more effective. Dysentery victims were given everything from whiskey and blackberry juice to turpentine and strychnine (a substance used for rat poison today). The standard treatment for malaria was a dose of whiskey and a drug called quinine. But medical records also show that physicians experimented with an unusual assortment of remedies, including cod-liver oil, ammonia, syrup of wild cherry, cream of tartar and cinnamon. Whatever the remedy, doctors usually prescribed enormous doses of it. Sometimes patients suffered more from the treatment than the illness itself.

These unreliable remedies did not help to improve the reputation of doctors within the regiments. Many soldiers chose to treat themselves rather than depend on the services of their physicians. "If a fellow has to [go to the] Hospital," declared one Union soldier, "you might as well say good bye." Such statements were rarely true. Most army physicians genuinely cared about their pa-

Soldiers at a hospital in Washington, D.C., some crippled for life, pose solemnly for the photographer. In Civil War general hospitals patients were housed in large open wards with 40 to 60 beds lining the walls.

tients and saved lives daily despite the poor medical knowledge of the time. As volunteer Katharine Wormeley revealed, "I am astonished at the cheerful devotion—whole-souled and whole-bodied devotion—of the surgeon and medical students attached to this boat. These young men toil day and night at the severest work, quick, intelligent, and tender."

The true test of the Civil War surgeon's abilities came after each battle, when hundreds of wounded soldiers were dragged into the crude, outdoor field hospitals for treatment. Here behind the bloody lines of the battlefield, the soldiers suffered the most. Some had been hit by the rifle bullets called minie balls, which splintered the bones of arms and legs like driftwood. Others had been caught in the path of cannon shells, and their wounds were deep and jagged. Tortured with pain, the soldiers often had to wait hours before a tired, overworked surgeon looked at their injuries. By this time, the dirty wounds had usually become infected.

The wait was even longer for wounded soldiers who had been captured by the enemy. Each army cared for its own injured troops before tending to its prisoners. John Dooley, the Confederate soldier who was shot through both thighs at Gettysburg, lay on the ground in agony for five days before his wounds were washed and bandaged by a Union doctor.

For many injured men, the nightmare began on the way to the outdoor hospitals located several miles from the battlefield. When the war opened, neither side had an efficient system for moving the wounded to the rear. The armies used stretcher bearers and bumpy two-wheeled carts known as "hop, step, and jumps" or "avalanches." Gradually, the Union Army established an ambulance corps of horse-drawn wagons. But even these vehicles were not a great improvement. When Dooley rode to the hospital, his wagon bounced and swayed over the rutted roads, jolting the wounded passengers inside. Throughout the entire trip, one soldier next to Dooley screamed in pain each time the ambulance bumped over a stone or ditch.

Many soldiers suffered more from thirst than the pain of their wounds. Sometimes water was so scarce in the makeshift hospitals that the surgeons could not wash after each operation. Without realizing they were spreading infection, the doctors rubbed their

Dressed in exotic Zouave uniforms, several soldiers pretend to be wounded while their comrades practice an ambulance drill. In a true battle, this scene would not have been so peaceful or organized. Ambulance workers often had to dodge bullets to reach their patients.

bloody hands on their aprons and wiped their instruments on the nearest rag. Nearby the patients cried out weakly for water, trying to be heard from their places on the ground. When a nurse finally brought Dooley some water, he refused to drink. It was warm and muddy, and reeked of rotting corpses. Rather than swallow this foul liquid, Dooley waited four days until someone was kind enough to give him a cup of fresh spring water.

The wounded endured more misery as they watched what happened to those who reached the operating table before them. The surgeons worked in plain view—on front porches, under trees, or in open tents. Two-thirds of their cases were patients whose arms or legs were so badly mangled that they had to be removed. Using an old door or wagon boards for an operating platform, the surgeons performed these grisly amputations with factory-line speed. First, they held a cloth soaked with an anaesthetic called chloroform over the patient's nose and mouth. But sometimes this drug was unavailable or simply not strong enough to put the patient to sleep. On these occasions, the surgeon ordered his assistants to hold down the squirming soldier while he pushed ahead with the operation.

Shrieks of pain rang through the woods around the outdoor hospitals. Passing soldiers who wandered over to the surgeon's tent to investigate stumbled upon a gruesome scene. As one private described: "A large hole was dug in the yard about the size of a small cellar, and into this the legs and arms were thrown as they were lopped off by the surgeons. . . . The day was hot and sultry, and the odor . . . was sickening in the extreme."

While amputations were the most feared procedure, any surgery during the Civil War was a horrible ordeal. Some doctors believed chloroform was unnecessary for soldiers who required no more than a bullet removed. Instead, they gave their patients a shot of whiskey and set to work. Although each surgeon's kit included special instruments for operating on gunshot wounds, the physicians preferred the faster technique of using their fingers to probe for bullets. As John Dooley learned, the consequences of this hurried method were dangerous. Several weeks after his operation, Dooley found fragments of cloth in his wound and still burned with fever from infection.

Like Dooley, most of those who survived their treatment in the field still faced a long and risky period of recovery. To begin this process, the injured men were quickly moved to a general hospital located in the nearest city. The soldiers who arrived at these hospitals expecting to find comfortable and orderly surroundings were usually disappointed. In one of the largest Confederate hospitals, whitewashed sheds served as the wards. At night

While a nurse looks on, wounded Federal soldiers attempt to make themselves comfortable behind a makeshift hospital in Virginia.

the patients could see the stars and watch the falling snow through the wide cracks in the roof.

This shelter was luxurious compared to the quarters where many wounded prisoners were housed. Although Dooley's injuries left him unable to walk for several weeks, he was not allowed to move into a hospital after his treatment in the field. Instead, the Union Army sent Dooley, along with other captured Confederates, directly to a prison at Fort McHenry in Baltimore, Maryland. To inmates, Fort McHenry was known as the "Black Hole." In his journal, Dooley described his first sight of this miserable guard-house: "Our ambulances halt before a row of low buildings which appeared somewhat like those in which I have seen cattle quartered. . . . Our settling down consists in spreading our blankets on the filthy floor, and although many of us are wounded severely enough to merit beds, but one or two are given even bunks, and these are glad enough to leave them to their former occupants—the vermin."

When the war began, neither side had any intention of treating its prisoners so cruelly. The huge number of captives, like the high rate of sick and wounded, surprised and overwhelmed the opposing governments. Desperate for space, they scrambled to convert whatever large buildings they could find into prisons—factories, warehouses, military barracks, jails, even schools. Finding food for the inmates was another grave problem. The armies, especially in the South, could not always feed their own soldiers, much less scores of enemy prisoners. Before each side determined how to improve the monstrous holding pens they had created, 56,000 inmates died of starvation and disease.

Thirteen thousand of these deaths occurred in an infamous Georgia prison called Andersonville. Federal captives began arriving at Andersonville in February 1864, while the high wall of pine logs surrounding the camp was still under construction. At first, the prisoners were relieved to find that this stockade would be their only barrier at Andersonville. Instead of dark and stifling guardhouses, there were twenty-five acres of open field. Those who did not have tents could build huts out of scraps of wood and canvas, vines, and pine boughs. And there was still plenty of room to move around, even as the number of inmates reached 7,500 in March.

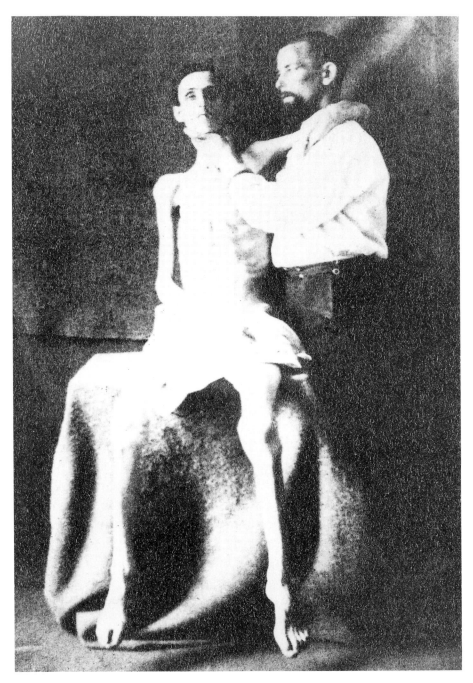

Too weak to sit upright on his own, an emaciated Federal soldier released from Richmond's Belle Isle Prison shows the hideous effects of his captivity. In several Civil War prisons it was common for inmates to receive no more than a spoonful of beans and a handful of corn meal each day.

But only five months later, the population of the camp leaped to 33,000. The wood for shelter and cooking fires had long since disappeared. The sun beat down and blistered the men in their tattered clothing. Andersonville had become disastrously overcrowded. "There was hardly room for all to lie down at night," wrote Cavalryman John McElroy from Illinois, "and to walk a few hundred feet in any direction would require an hour's patient threading through the mass of men and tents."

Everywhere that Private McElroy looked, there was suffering. During the last sweltering weeks of July, the scene around his tent was unforgettable. Directly in front of McElroy, two brothers lay side by side, dying from scurvy. This disease, brought on by months without fruits and vegetables, had caused the brothers to lose their teeth and hair. The bones of their face, arms, ribs, and thighs jutted out, making them look more like skeletons than living humans. To the right of McElroy, a young sergeant paced back and forth, holding the unbandaged stump of his amputated arm. To his left, a prisoner who had been driven insane by the tortures at Andersonville played a flute night and day. Even when the other exasperated soldiers shouted insults and threw stones at the crazy man, he still would not stop playing his mournful tunes.

With such unbearable surroundings, many prisoners could think of nothing but escape. In the seven months that McElroy was locked in Andersonville, he and a secret society of fellow inmates made five attempts to sneak beyond the well-guarded stockade walls. Each of these efforts failed, mainly because members of the group turned into traitors and exposed the escape plots to the Confederate guards. By serving as spies, these inmates could gain favor with the rebels and receive clothes, extra rations, or heavy-duty tents.

Not all escape plans were unsuccessful. On February 4, 1864, a group of exhausted captives finished digging a tunnel to freedom underneath Richmond's Libby Prison for Federal officers. For weeks Colonel Thomas E. Rose of the Seventy-seventh Pennsylvania had supervised the tedious work. At first glance, the scheme seemed impossible. To reach freedom, the inmates needed to dig a passageway from the basement of the prison to the other side of a fence fifty feet away—all without being detected. The tunnel

At Andersonville in Georgia, there was not one tree to shade the ragged shelters and prisoners from the brutal August sun. The water provided by the prison camp brought little relief. Captives had to collect their bathing and drinking water from a foul stream known as Sweet Water Branch that ran alongside the trench latrine.

needed to be large and stable enough for a man to crawl through on his stomach. Yet the prisoners' only tools were a table knife, an old chisel, a wooden box, some string, and a few candles.

In their frenzy to be free, the prisoners found ways to overcome these tremendous obstacles. They took turns burrowing through the tunnel with two men working at a time. While one man entered the hole with the tools and scooped dirt into the box, another fanned air into the passageway with his hat and pulled out boxloads of earth with the string. After countless hours of digging night and day, Rose finally announced that the breakout was ready to begin.

To conceal the escape, the inmates held a loud and rowdy musical show. While guards listened to the boisterous songs upstairs, one prisoner after another squeezed into the cramped passageway in the basement and groped toward the tunnel opening. From the upstairs windows, the inmates could see Rose and the other escapees emerge on the Richmond streets. A wave of panicky excitement swept through the prison. Dozens of officers scrambled to the basement to join the breakout. Amazingly, it was not until morning roll call that the guards discovered 109 men were missing.

Within minutes, the Confederates were ringing churchbells, forming search parties, and sending out packs of dogs. Of the officers who escaped, forty-eight were recaptured and two drowned trying to swim to safety. Colonel Thomas Rose was among the unfortunate men dragged back to Libby and placed in solitary confinement.

Less than one year later, Colonel Thomas Rose again left Libby Prison, but this time no one challenged his right to freedom. In early 1865, the North and South signed a prisoner exchange agreement. This contract allowed the armies to trade enlisted men and officers of equal rank on a one-for-one basis. However, by 1865, an agreement was not even necessary to free prisoners. Peace was on the way. Neither side fought to hold their captives any longer. All across the North and the South, guards stood back while lines of inmates joyfully filed out of open prison gates. On February 27, Confederate John Dooley wrote this triumphant entry in his diary: "Two hundred prisoners leave and one hundred more

A group of Union prisoners scheduled to be exchanged for their southern counterparts await their release. By the time inmates were freed, many wore nothing but tatters. At Andersonville, some prisoners were forced to cut and sew their tents into clothing.

to go today and I am among the number—GLORY ALLELUIA!"

For many prisoners, freedom came too late. As Dooley sailed to his home state of Virginia after nearly two years in captivity, his steamer glided alongside another boat loaded with Confederate ex-prisoners. On the decks Dooley could see the covered bodies of twenty men who had died during the voyage to Richmond. The remaining passengers, with their sunken eyes and stooped shoulders, were suffering from months of starvation and neglect. They barely had enough strength to step onto the pier. "Poor fellows!" Dooley wrote. "How anxious they are to reach once more southern soil. See! The most emaciated among them spring forward with a light step as if they could walk for miles in such a cause; but exhausted by their efforts they fall and have to be conveyed in ambulances." Many of these men had survived the horrors of prison camps only to die on their two-day journey back home.

Many boys who fell below the age limit for enlisting could not resist the urge to follow their fathers and older brothers to war. Like the young soldier pictured here with an injured arm, some returned to service even after being wounded.

FIVE

The Patchwork Armies

During their weeks in camp, battle, and prison, the soldiers discovered more than the ugly side of war. Many discovered that they knew very little about the nation and the people they were fighting for. The majority of Civil War recruits were white farmers, raised in small towns or country villages. For these men, who had rarely explored beyond the nearest city, the wide assortment of personalities and cultures represented in the ranks came as a fascinating surprise.

New York volunteer Frank Moran spent several months trapped in the cramped rooms of Libby Prison with 1,200 other captives. There he could not help but mingle with the diverse range of men who made up the Union Army. "Libby Prison was a vast museum of human character, where the chances of war had brought into close communion every type and temperament," Moran observed. "There were men of all sizes and nationalities. Youth and age, and titled men of Europe, who had enlisted in our cause, might be found among the captives. There were about thirty doctors, as many ministers, a score of journalists and lawyers, a few actors. . . . All in all, Libby prison, from the vast mixture of its inmates . . . was doubtless the best school of human nature ever seen in this country."

In both the North and the South, most soldiers fell between the ages of eighteen and twenty-nine. But also scattered among the ranks were hundreds of volunteers who did not meet the minimum age requirement of eighteen. Some boys were so anxious to enlist that they lied outright about their age. Others felt pangs of guilt about deceiving recruitment officers. To ease their worries, a few clever boys wrote the number eighteen on slips of paper, which they placed inside their shoes. When the officer asked their age, they could cheerfully and truthfully reply, "I'm over eighteen."

Many boys enrolled in the army as trumpeters or drummers since there were no strict age requirements for musicians. But some youngsters still had problems joining the service. The captain of a Michigan regiment rejected twelve-year-old Robert Henry Hendershot as a drummer boy, claiming he was too small. Refusing to stay at home, Hendershot hid in a toolbox on the train that was carrying the Michigan troops to the front. When the captain discovered the boy in Indiana, he gave him a stern spanking and bought him a ticket on the next train back home. Still, Hendershot would not give up his dreams of marching with the soldiers to victory. Once he had escaped from the baggage master, he caught another train and followed the regiment to its next stop. Hendershot was high in the branches of a persimmon tree, picking fruit for the soldiers, when he was discovered for the second time. Instead of listening to the furious captain's lectures, the boy promptly found the commander of a different company and offered his services as a drummer. Finally, Hendershot's stubborn nature was rewarded. He served in the U.S. Army for the next four years.

Drummer boys like Hendershot often performed other chores besides beating time to marches and drills. In between their musical duties, they frequently brought water to the soldiers, worked as barbers and cooks, sharpened the surgeon's instruments, or carried stretchers. When fighting broke out, no one tried to shelter the young boys from violent or bloody scenes. In fact, many doctors recruited drummers as medical assistants. With white handkerchiefs tied around their arms to signal their noncombat role, the youngsters scurried around the makeshift field hospitals, following the surgeons' orders. Some boys were called upon to assist in the gruesome amputations. George T. Ulmer, a sixteen-year-old

Young men, many still teenagers, lined up at the recruiting stations. This youthful Michigan recruit poses proudly in his plaid flannel shirt, brandishing his hunting knife from home.

When the time to march into battle finally arrived, drummer boys such as these signaled the troops with a drum beat known as *the long roll*.

drummer from Maine, explained how he helped to administer chloroform: "It was a horrible task at first. My duty was to hold the sponge of ether to the face of the soldier who was to be operated on and to stand there and see the surgeons cut and saw legs and arms as if they were cutting swine or sheep. . . . At intervals, when the pile became large, I was obliged to take a load of legs and arms and place them in a trench nearby for burial."

Many young musicians could not resist the urge to trade their drums and trumpets for muskets and join the fighting. John Lincoln Clem, who ran away from home at the age of nine to drum for an Ohio regiment, became famous for his bravery in battle. During one fierce engagement, Clem picked up a musket just in time to prevent being captured. When an enemy officer charged at Clem and demanded his surrender, the boy shot the Confederate off his horse. This was only the start of Clem's bold exploits. After being promoted to the rank of sergeant at the age of twelve, he fought in six more battles and ended the war as a messenger for the Union Army. As one officer in the Ohio artillery described this legendary youngster to his family, "He rides around on horseback with a great pistol hung out his side after the fashion of a mounted orderly and considering how much is made of him, he doesn't seem to put on many airs."

Not all boys who saw action lived to become legends. Like older soldiers, these volunteers were often cut down by bullets, disease, or too many wearing weeks in prison. But when young boys died at war, the troops felt unusually sad. These deaths seemed to remind even the most hardened veterans of the wastefulness of war. At a funeral for a young drummer from New York, one spectator noticed the reactions of the members in his regiment. "As the coffin was taken from the drummer's quarters . . . many a man, who would not flinch on the field of battle, shed tears over the remains of poor Clarence. He was the smallest in the corps and liked by everyone who knew him."

Boys were not the only soldiers who lied about their age to be accepted in the army. While the War Department in 1862 passed a law against enlisting volunteers over age forty-five, many men in their fifties and sixties found their way into the ranks. The oldest soldier of the war was Curtis King, who joined the Thirty-seventh Iowa Infantry at the age of eighty. King's regiment, which was nicknamed the Graybeards, became well-known for its large number of elderly recruits. More than 145 men in the unit were over sixty years of age. But like Private King, most of these volunteers did not make strong soldiers. Frequently, they had to be discharged from duty within a few months because of medical problems or their difficulty in keeping up with younger troops.

One diverse group of soldiers that strengthened the armies, especially in the North, was the force of volunteers from foreign nations. Of some two million men who served on the Union side, half a million had been born overseas. Many of these immigrants had come to the United States ten or twenty years before the Civil War began, hoping to escape poverty and oppression in Europe. America offered jobs, acres of land to develop, and the opportunity to improve one's future. Most foreigners moved to the United States never expecting that war would break out. But when the Union and Confederacy sounded the call for volunteers, thousands of immigrants joined the army for many of the same reasons that native-born men did. They liked the prospect of steady wages, adventure, and the chance to fight for an important cause.

Native-born soldiers did not always welcome foreign recruits into their ranks. Many either mistreated or completely avoided these newcomers, whose habits seemed outlandish and strange. When the Scotsmen of the Seventy-ninth New York paraded into Washington wearing their traditional kilts, American volunteers viciously ridiculed these "soldiers in skirts." After enduring insults for several days, all but one proud Scotsman in the regiment had given up wearing kilts in the city streets.

Southern soldiers were even more intolerant of immigrant recruits than troops in the North. While 25 percent of the Union forces came from foreign countries, only 9 percent of the Confederate armies were foreign-born. Southerners had fewer opportunities to become acquainted with these mysterious men from abroad. One Texas private expressed a common viewpoint among his American comrades when he wrote, "There was a mess in my company made up exclusively of foreigners. They were a selfish set and the boys had little to do with them. Their names were so everlastingly long that the orderly sergeant could never pronounce them at roll call."

Faced with such attitudes, many immigrants preferred joining units made up of their own countrymen. In the North, the number of all-German regiments ran into the dozens. The Irish, who were the second largest group of foreigners in the Union, composed the majority of at least twenty regiments. Some units were a hodgepodge of nationalities. The colorful Thirty-ninth New York included Hungarian, Spanish, Italian, French, English, and German recruits.

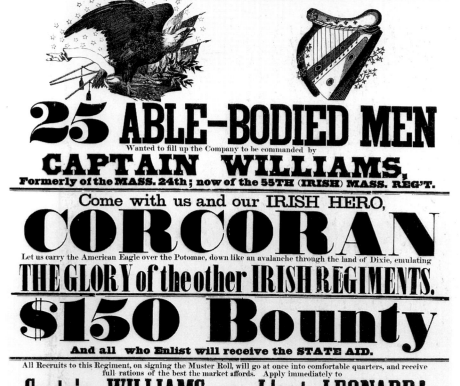

THIRD IRISH REGIMENT

From Massachusetts, and First Irish Regiment for Nine Months' Service.

25 ABLE-BODIED MEN

Wanted to fill up the Company to be commanded by

CAPTAIN WILLIAMS,

Formerly of the MASS. 24th; now of the 55TH (IRISH) MASS. REG'T.

Come with us and our IRISH HERO,

CORCORAN

Let us carry the American Eagle over the Potomac, down like an avalanche through the land of Dixie, emulating

THE GLORY of the other IRISH REGIMENTS.

$150 Bounty

And all who Enlist will receive the STATE AID.

All Recruits to this Regiment, on signing the Muster Roll, will go at once into comfortable quarters, and receive full rations of the best the market affords. Apply immediately to

Captain WILLIAMS, or, Lieut. LEONARD!

No. 109 CAMBRIDGE STREET, BOSTON.

Herald Job Office, No. 4 Williams Court, Boston.

This Federal recruitment poster lures Irishmen into nine months of service by promising a cash reward, comfortable quarters, and full meals. Such recruiting efforts were successful; some 150,000 Irish-born men joined the ranks.

In order to lead this bewildering mix of men, officers of the regiment had to conduct paperwork and drill in six different languages.

One group of American-born soldiers practiced customs that were much more exotic than those of European volunteers. American Indians also left their mark on the roll of Civil War soldiers. Listed among the names of recruits who fought in the

The most famous of all Indians in the Civil War was Cherokee leader Stand Watie. Watie, who reached the rank of brigadier general, did not surrender his troops until a full month after all other southern forces had laid down their arms.

West are Captain Spring Frog, John Bearmeat, Crying Bear, Alex Scarce Water, and Warkiller Hogshooter.

While the Indians maintained a reputation as strong fighters, they never adapted well to the rigid discipline of the military. For men who had spent their lives freely roaming the frontier, it was agonizing to stand at attention, march in formation, and obey the officers' constant orders. Some Indians also refused to wear the standard uniforms. One Confederate, who watched a group of Cherokee recruits ride into battle, described the Indians' unsoldierly dress: "They came trotting by our camp on their little Indian ponies, yelling forth their wild whoop. . . . Their faces were painted, and their long straight hair tied in a queue, hung down behind. Their dress was chiefly in the Indian costume—buckskin hunting shirts, dyed of almost every color, leggings and moccasins. . . . Many of them were bareheaded and about half carried only bows and arrows, tomahawks and war-clubs."

The Indians' style of carrying out orders was often as unconventional as their clothing. When a Federal captain instructed a patrol of Indians to help him destroy several Confederate supply houses in Mississippi, the soldiers overstepped their duties and ravaged the town. "No sooner had they comprehended the nature of the work we had to do," the captain wrote, "than they 'put their war paint on,' and with demoniac yells and all sorts of leapings and wild motions began putting the torch to every house they came to." Fire engines were called to put out the flames that the Indians had set in homes and churches, but the frenzied soldiers tried to stop the firemen's work by ripping open the hoses with their bayonets. In desperation, the captain finally summoned a company of whites to round up the Indians and escort them back to their quarters.

Considering the degrading treatment they received from most officers, Indian soldiers performed better in the military than their commanders had a right to expect. Native American troops frequently did not receive enough pay, food, clothing or weapons. Even when the armies tried to send supplies to the Indians, officers often gave these precious goods to white soldiers instead.

No group of recruits encountered more prejudice than black Americans. Even in the North, where slavery had been outlawed, the majority of whites still believed that blacks were inferior human beings. The idea of enlisting blacks as soldiers appalled most Union citizens during the first days of war. They argued that arming blacks might threaten whites' power over the darker race and lead to a huge rebellion. Some recruits swore they would never fight alongside black men. In a letter to his wife, one Federal volunteer even hinted that he would rather let the Confederates win the war than put blacks in uniform. "The Southern people are rebels to the government, but they are white," he wrote, "and God never intended [blacks] to put white people down."

But as the war dragged on, these protests softened. The Union began to face a severe shortage of soldiers in the summer of 1862. Meanwhile, human rights supporters and abolitionists were putting increasing pressure on President Lincoln and the Congress to reinforce the ranks with blacks. The well-known former slave and black leader Frederick Douglass pleaded, "Give them a chance. I don't say that they will fight better than other men. All I say is, Give them a chance!" The chance for blacks finally came on New Year's Day in 1863 when Lincoln signed the Emancipation Proclamation. This document officially declared the end of slavery across the South. As thousands of freed slaves left their masters and came pouring across the Union lines, leaders in Washington realized that these refugees represented an immense supply of manpower. By the spring of 1863, the North was openly encouraging the recruitment of black regiments.

Yet the chance to wear a uniform and carry a musket did not always guarantee black soldiers time in battle. Many high-ranking officers preferred to assign black troops to permanent labor and save their white regiments for combat. Day after day black recruits watched white soldiers lounging in camp or marching into battle while they dug trenches, built roads, and buried corpses. One black regiment was called in for burial duty after the corpses had baked under the hot June sun for ten days. Because they had to work dangerously close to the Confederate lines, the soldiers had no choice but to dig the graves at night. Amid complete darkness and the awful stench, they groped around for the rotting bodies, not daring to make a sound. Naturally, blacks bitterly resented such unfair assignments, believing they were being reduced to slavery once more. A private working in a Louisiana swamp protested, "Instead of the musket, it is the spade and the wheelbarrow and the axe." Another soldier declared, "Slavery with all its horrors can not [equal] this, for it is nothing but work from morning 'til night."

When blacks did get the chance to see combat, they surprised white soldiers and officers with their heroic performances. Colonel Robert Gould Shaw was one of the few white commanders who were convinced that his black regiment could prove itself in battle. On July 18, 1863, the twenty-five-year-old colonel volunteered the men of the Fifty-fourth Massachusetts Infantry to lead an attack on Fort Wagner, a Confederate stronghold guarding the entrance to Charleston Harbor. For the recruits of the Fifty-fourth, this mission presented a frightening number of challenges. Only a portion of the men had ever faced the enemy before—and this had happened just once, two days earlier. To make matters more difficult, the regiment had been on the march for the past two days without food. Now a mile of beach, a waist-deep moat, and a mountain of sand and logs lay between the weary troops and victory. But after months of waiting to show their worth in battle, the men were determined to rush ahead and capture the Confederate fort.

At twilight, Colonel Shaw threw down his cigar and took his position at the head of the regiment. "Move in quick time until within a hundred yards of the fort," Shaw commanded, "then, double-quick and charge!" As the men churned their way through the surf and sand, the guns of five surrounding forts opened a brutal fire. But "not a man flinched, though it was a trying time," wrote survivor Sergeant Major Lewis Douglass, the son of Frederick Douglass. "A shell would explode and clear a space of twenty feet, our men would close up again."

The black soldiers pushed on desperately, increasing speed until they were running through the showers of exploding shells and sand. Colonel Shaw had just reached the top of the rebel encampment and shouted to his men to move forward, when a ball crashed into his chest. Still, the survivors dashed forward. For a brief moment the Union flag waved on the parapet as the soldiers swarmed into the fort and lunged at the Confederates with their

Thousands of slaves who escaped to freedom in the North worked for Union forces as servants and laborers. They received a small wage for their services.

bayonets. But the men of the Fifty-fourth were far outnumbered and their supporting troops arrived too late to offer any aid. They fell back, leaving behind nearly half of their ranks dead, wounded, or captured.

While the Fifty-fourth's charge on Fort Wagner was a military failure, it was a triumph for black soldiers. In the face of overwhelming danger, these men had fought with courage and a willingness to die for the freedom of their race. Their bravery swayed the minds of the northern people and helped to clear the way for 180,000 black recruits to serve in the Union Army. Intending to insult whites in the North, the Confederates had buried Colonel Shaw in a pit with his black comrades. Instead, this gesture turned the gravesite into a symbol of the colonel's honorable struggle. When Shaw's father learned that officials were trying to retrieve the remains, he requested that his son's body stay with his men. "We hold that a soldier's most appropriate burial-place," he stated, "is on the field where he has fallen."

The Union's success with black regiments put pressure on the Confederacy to turn to its own slaves for military help. Even after Lincoln issued his Emancipation Proclamation, thousands of blacks remained on the plantations. Surprisingly, many Southern black men were willing to risk their lives for the Confederate cause. But each time this debate arose, the majority of citizens voiced their disapproval. The idea grated against everything that Southerners had ever known. The president of the Confederacy, Jefferson Davis himself, declared that all white Federal officers of black regiments who were taken prisoner would be sentenced to death. After several battles, witnesses reported seeing Confederates ruthlessly massacre captured black soldiers.

But as the South's efforts to win the war grew more desperate, the Confederate Congress reluctantly passed a law in March 1865 calling for the enlistment of 300,000 black soldiers. An all-black unit was quickly organized in Richmond. When the proud troops marched through the streets in their new uniforms, the white crowds threw mud and yelled insults at the soldiers. The war ended before the southern black volunteers were allowed to join in battle and prove themselves as soldiers instead of slaves.

The exceptional performance of blacks in battle finally brought them acceptance as American soldiers. After one engagement, a southern officer reported that his attack "was resisted by the negro portion of the enemy's force, while the white portion . . . ran like whipped curs almost as soon as the charge was ordered."

General Robert E. Lee, the commander of all Confederate forces, was extremely popular with his men. After signing the surrender papers in the quiet village of Appomattox, Virginia, the general rode through the ranks on his gray horse, Traveller. One weeping soldier shouted, "I love you just as well as ever, General Lee."

SIX

The Long Road Home

On April 9, 1865, the Confederate commander, General Robert E. Lee, emerged from a Virginia farmhouse, where the outcome of the Civil War had finally been decided. As Lee rode slowly into the southern lines, a crowd of soldiers surrounded him. "Are we surrendered?" someone cried out. The general did not answer, but the truth was plain from his expression. An hour later, on the way to his headquarters, Lee passed by more men who had gathered along the road, waiting to hear the news. The soldiers cheered wildly when they spotted their beloved commander, but then they noticed tears in Lee's eyes. All along the road, men threw themselves on the ground, covered their faces with their hands, and wept. Even officers sat on their horses and sobbed. As Lee reached his tent, he finally spoke. "Men, we have fought through the war together," he said, with tears trickling down his cheeks. "I have done the best I could for you. My heart is too full to say more."

Although the South's surrender saddened the soldiers, it did not surprise them. By the spring of 1865, the Confederates were exhausted, starving, and fighting without shirts and shoes. They stumbled through battles, hopelessly worn down by the more powerful Union Army. Secretly, many soldiers knew they were fighting for a lost cause. But some stubbornly held on out of devotion to their leaders. Others could not stand the thought of giving up after investing four long years of hardship in the struggle. Surrender, they believed, would mean all of their efforts had been a waste.

Not all Confederates reacted to surrender with dismay. There were also soldiers who quietly accepted defeat, glad to be ending the bloodshed for good. Several minutes after hearing the announcement, they began to talk of the fastest way to get home.

Not far from the southern camp where Lee delivered his message, the Federal soldiers were also receiving the news. As soon as the Union commander, General Ulysses S. Grant, had signed the surrender documents, one of his staff members jumped on a horse and set off at a gallop. For several minutes the usually gruff officer forgot his stern ways. He charged into camp, waving his hat and beaming with excitement. "It's all over, boys!" he yelled gleefully. "Lee's surrendered! It's all over!" A volunteer vividly remembered the scene: "The men listen for a moment," he recalled, "and then up to the heavens goes such a shout as none of them will ever hear again. . . . The air is black with hats and boots, coats, knapsacks, shirts and cartridge-boxes. . . . They fall on each other's necks and laugh and cry by turns. Huge, lumbering bearded men embrace and kiss like schoolgirls, then dance and sing and shout, stand on their heads and play at leap frog."

For some Federals, victory was bittersweet. In the midst of their rejoicing, they could not help feeling a rush of respect and pity for their opponents. In the Virginia battle that signaled the end for the once great Confederate Army, a Union soldier described the moment when the white flag of truce rose over the enemy lines. Instead of giving their usual victory cheer, the Federals stared across the battlefield silently, unable to believe that the ordeal was finally over. "I remember how we sat there," wrote the soldier, "and pitied and sympathized with these courageous southern men who had fought for four long and dreary years all so stubbornly, so bravely and so well, and now, whipped, beaten, completely used up, were fully at our mercy—it was pitiful, sad, hard, and seemed to us altogether too bad."

When Ulysses S. Grant finally became the Union commander in 1864, he plunged into his task with confidence and natural military skill—traits that had been missing in the string of Federal commanders before him. As one fellow officer commented, Grant wore "an expression as if he had determined to drive his head through a brick wall, and was about to do it."

During a discussion of the surrender terms in the McLean house at Appomattox, General Lee informed General Grant that his men had been living on parched corn for the past few days. Grant generously agreed to send rations for 25,000 through the Confederate lines.

But most Federals were too caught up in their country's celebrations to feel this sadness for long. Weeks after the surrender the Union was still holding victory parades and ceremonies. All across the North soldiers returned home to brass bands and crowded receptions. The most magnificent of these spectacles was the Grand Review in Washington, D.C. For two days in May, veteran Union soldiers marched in rows of sixty down the city's main avenue. This parade was nothing like the farewell marches of 1861. Instead of the colorful mismatch of new uniforms, the sunburned veterans wore faded and ragged blue. They carried dusty flags shredded by gunfire. One brigade brought along the treasures

During the war soldiers ate, slept, drilled, and fought side by side. Although they were overjoyed by the prospect of peace, many soldiers hated saying goodbye to their wartime comrades.

On May 23 and 24, 1865, Union armies paraded up Pennsylvania Avenue in Washington, D.C., for a final Grand Review. Under the shade of elm trees on the sidelines, veterans who had been disabled in battle watched solemnly from crutches and chairs.

of its foraging missions in the South: pack mules, live chickens, herds of cows and sheep, and wagons piled with household goods. Behind the soldiers trooped families of freed slaves.

Homecoming was much different for soldiers in the South. The trip only deepened the sorrow and resentment for most Confederates. Before they could see their families, the soldiers faced the difficult task of traveling through their war-torn region. The Federals had destroyed vital railroad lines in their march across the South, leaving behind miles of tangled steel. And so, thousands of Confederates were forced to straggle home by foot, one-by-one or in little bands. On their journey, the soldiers began to

Four forlorn children appear lost in the rubble of Charleston, South Carolina. After stubbornly withstanding hammering attacks from the Union Army and Navy, the city finally fell in February 1865.

realize how badly four years of invasion and poverty had crippled the South. They passed the blackened ruins of cities such as Richmond, Virginia, where homeless citizens wandered through the still smoking streets. In the countryside, cotton fields were choked with weeds and plantation homes stood empty with sagging porches and doors hanging from their hinges.

Lack of money made traveling even more difficult for the southern veterans. While the Union presented its soldiers with generous amounts in salary and back pay, the Confederacy did not have funds to pay all the wages it owed. Some penniless Southerners had to beg for room and board with nothing to exchange except the gloomy news of the surrender. "All I desire is to get home, and I am so worried all day about the means," John Dooley wrote wearily in his diary. "Never before have I felt so much distress of mind and never have I felt so utterly abandoned. . . . Where others feel perfectly at home boarding at the expense of others, I am perfectly miserable lest I am unwelcome and a burden."

When the footsore rebels at last reached their hometowns, they received a disappointing welcome. There were no speeches and parades to greet the Confederates. Throughout the deep South, in isolated regions left untouched by the damages of war, citizens were shocked by word of the surrender. The townspeople of Selma, Alabama, first treated returning Confederates like quitters—until they later learned their soldiers had fought longer than anyone had a right to expect. In other areas closer to the battle zones, some rebels found problems more serious than failing crops and missing livestock when they arrived at their homesteads. Frequently they discovered that their wives and children had fled from the threat of the invading army, leaving no message about where they had gone.

One way or another, most soldiers were finally reunited with their families. For months volunteers on both sides had been dreaming of this moment. In many cases, the homecomings were just as dramatic as the soldiers had imagined. In August 1865, a young man from Maine, William Archibald, returned from war. When he arrived unannounced at the front gate, his mother cried, "Is it you, Willie?" and fainted in his arms. Once his family had recovered from the surprise, William entertained the group with tales of his soldiering days. By the light of the coal-oil lamp in the parlor, he demonstrated how his rifle was loaded and unloaded. Then he passed around his six-shooter, belt, and sword. To all those in the room, twenty-three-year-old William was a hero.

At first the veterans felt nothing but delight over this extra attention and the comforts of their new-found freedom. "Our soldier life had come to an end," a Connecticut private wrote after three years of service. "No more picket and guard duty. No more marching by day and night. . . . No more camp life, sleeping on the ground in all kinds of weather. No more the long roll to call us out into the night. No more the danger of battle, sickness, or suffering from hunger and thirst." But despite the bliss of independence, the veterans quickly realized that their experiences in the military were not so easy to leave behind. On his first night at home William Archibald could not fall asleep in his boyhood room. His old feather bed felt soft and suffocating, and it creaked whenever he moved. After an hour of tossing and rearranging the covers, the young man got up and tried the floor. It felt hard, cool, and familiar, and before long he was asleep.

When the excitement over their arrival died away, the veterans faced a new challenge—the task of resuming the lives they had led before the war. "I have almost a dread of being a citizen, of trying to be sharp and trying to make money," one Union man confessed in his diary upon his dismissal from the service. "I don't think I dread the work . . . but I am sure that civil life will go sorely against the grain for a time." The veterans felt strangely out of place among their acquaintances and childhood friends who had stayed home during the war. Months of encountering death and hardship had given former soldiers a different, more serious outlook on life. Their families were usually the first to notice the change. As one southern wife observed about her husband, "Calhoun is . . . much more sober than he used to be. . . . I do not see that he has changed very much in character except that [he] is graver."

Many veterans quickly grew restless in their new surroundings. It was difficult to settle down to the ordinary routine of farm chores and factory work after the thrilling escapades of the army.

During the war, artists created romantic images of the wounded soldier's joyous homecoming. In reality, many veterans returned to find their homes looted, crops failing, and families gone.

And compared to the perilous situations on the battlefield, the humdrum problems that arose at home seemed trivial. A large number of ex-soldiers suddenly found their old jobs too confining and sought out more exciting careers. Soon after the war, Private Leander Stillwell decided to put away his plow and pursue a degree in law. Other veterans roamed to the frontiers of the West, searching for fortune and adventure.

While the veterans searched for harmony in their new lives, making peace with their former enemies often seemed like an impossible feat. For years after the war, the South boiled with resentment of the "dirty Yankees." A North Carolina man, who claimed the Federals had killed his sons, burned his house, and stolen his slaves, declared, "I git up at half-past four in the morning, and sit up till twelve at night, to hate 'em."

Despite their victory, the northern veterans also felt hatred. One tragic event following the surrender only served to deepen their wounds. Less than one week after Lee and Grant met in Virginia, an actor named John Wilkes Booth strode into the President's box at Ford's Theatre in Washington and shot Abraham Lincoln. The next day Lincoln died. Many Northerners wrongly believed that the murder was part of the Confederate government's plot to make a final stand against the Union. Confederates did not always help to change these beliefs. "I am glad of it!" cried one southern veteran from his bed in a Union hospital. "He won't free any more niggers." If the wardmaster had not intervened, the Federal patients would have beaten the rebel into silence.

Time alone could heal the ugly scars of the war. More than 600,000 soldiers had lost their lives in the vast conflict. Thousands more had been permanently crippled by their misfortunes in battle. But as time passed, the hideous memories faded deeper and deeper into the background. Ex-soldiers were the first to forgive. Each year the aging veterans gathered with their old comrades to march through city streets and tell stories of brave and daring deeds. Soon pleasant thoughts of patriotism and friendship overshadowed the darker impressions of war. And in a spirit of goodwill, veterans began to invite their old opponents to meet on friendly ground.

In 1888, on the twenty-fifth anniversary of the Battle of Gettysburg, men from both sides came together on the field where 50,000 soldiers had been killed, wounded or captured. Those who had once attacked one another with bullets and bayonets now walked across the battleground arm in arm. Among the last entries in his Civil War diary, a veteran from Maine expressed the ordinary soldier's quiet wish to leave the bitterness behind: "It is all over now. . . . the Rebel yell and the Yankee hurrah have all passed away and we again return to peace."

A Confederate veteran and a Union veteran clasp hands at a gathering of former soldiers a number of years after the war.

Glossary

---

artillery a branch of the armed forces that specializes in the use of large, mounted guns, which are too heavy to carry and are operated by specially trained crews

bayonet a long, narrow-bladed knife designed to fit on the end of a rifle barrel and be used in close combat

brigade a military combat unit. During the Civil War, a brigade consisted of approximately four regiments or four thousand men.

casualty one who is injured, killed, captured, or missing in action against an enemy

cavalry a branch of the army made up of troops trained to fight on horseback

Confederate States of America the alliance of eleven southern states that withdrew from the United States in 1860 and 1861. These states included Alabama, Arkansas, Florida, Georgia, Louisiana, Mississippi, North Carolina, South Carolina, Tennessee, Texas, and Virginia.

deserter one who leaves the armed forces without permission and has no intention of returning

draft   the government's selection of citizens for a required period of military service

Federal   having to do with the union of states that recognized the authority of the central United States government based in Washington, D.C.

hardtack   a hard biscuit or bread made only of flour and water

immigrant   one who leaves a country to settle permanently in another

infantry   the branch of the army made up of units trained to fight on foot

latrine   an outdoor toilet used by a barracks or camp

memoir   an account of incidents that the writer has experienced

picket   one or more soldiers who stand guard to give warning of enemy approach

regiment   a military unit of ground troops. In Civil War times, a regiment consisted of approximately one thousand soldiers, typically from the same state.

scurvy   a disease caused by lack of vitamin C, marked by soft and bleeding gums, bleeding under the skin, and extreme weakness

Union   another name for the United States of America, used especially during the Civil War. Sixteen out of thirty-three states remained loyal to the Union during the war.

vermin   any insects or small animals, such as cockroaches and rats, that are destructive, annoying, or harmful to health

Zouave   a member of any group patterned after the famous French infantry soldiers who wore colorful oriental uniforms and specialized in precision drilling

Bibliography

Beatty, John. *Memoirs of a Volunteer, 1861–1863*. Edited by Harvey S. Ford. New York: W. W. Norton & Company, n.d.

Bishop, Eleanor C. *Ponies, Patriots and Powder Monkeys: A History of Children in America's Armed Forces, 1776–1916*. Del Mar, Calif.: The Bishop Press, 1982.

Burton, William L. *Melting Pot Soldiers: The Union's Ethnic Regiments*. Ames: Iowa State University Press, 1988.

Carter, Robert Goldthwaite. *Four Brothers in Blue*. Austin: University of Texas Press, 1913.

Clemson, Floride. *A Rebel Came Home*. Edited by Charles M. McGee, Jr. Columbia: University of South Carolina Press, 1961.

Commager, Henry Steele, ed. *The Blue and the Gray: The Story of the Civil War as Told by Participants* (Vols. 1 and 2). New York: The Bobbs-Merrill Company, 1950.

Cornish, Dudley Taylor. *The Sable Arm: Negro Troops in the Union Army, 1861–1865*. New York: W. W. Norton & Company, 1966.

Davis, William C. *The Image of War, 1861–1865* (Vols. 1–6). Garden City, N.Y.: Doubleday & Company, 1982.

Dooley, John. *John Dooley, Confederate Soldier: His War Journal*. Edited by Joseph T. Durkin. Washington, D.C.: Georgetown University Press, 1945.

Glatthaar, Joseph T. *Forged in Battle: The Civil War Alliance of Black Soldiers and White Officers*. New York: The Free Press, 1990.

Gragg, Rod. *The Illustrated Confederate Reader*. New York: Harper & Row, 1989.

Ketchum, Richard M., ed. *The American Heritage Picture History of the Civil War*. New York: American Heritage Publishing Company, 1960.

Leech, Margaret. *Reveille in Washington, 1860–1865*. New York: Harper & Brothers, 1941.

McCarthy, Carlton. *Detailed Minutiae of Soldier Life in the Army of Northern Virginia, 1861–1865*. Richmond, Va.: Carlton McCarthy and Company, 1882.

McElroy, John. *Andersonville: A Story of Rebel Military Prisons*. Toledo, N.Y.: D. R. Locke, 1879.

McKim, Randolph H. *A Soldier's Recollections: Leaves from the Diary of a Young Confederate*. London: Longmans, Green, and Company, 1910.

Meltzer, Milton, ed. *Voices from the Civil War: A Documentary History of the Great American Conflict*. New York: Thomas Y. Crowell, 1989.

Norton, Oliver Willcox. *Army Letters, 1861–1865*. Chicago: O. W. Norton, 1903.

Palmer, Bruce. *First Bull Run: The Nation Wakes to War*. New York: The Macmillan Company, 1965.

Patterson, Edmund DeWitt. *Yankee Rebel: The Civil War Journal of Edmund DeWitt Patterson*. Edited by John G. Barrett. Chapel Hill: University of North Carolina Press, 1966.

Robertson, James I., Jr. *Soldiers Blue and Gray*. Columbia: University of South Carolina Press, 1988.

——————. *Tenting Tonight. The Soldier's Life* (Time-Life American Civil War Series). Alexandria, Va.: Time-Life Books, 1984.

Silliker, Ruth L., ed. *The Rebel Yell & The Yankee Hurrah: The Civil War Journal of a Maine Volunteer*. Camden, Maine: Down East Books, n.d.

Small, Abner R. *The Road to Richmond: The Civil War Memoirs of Major Abner R. Small*. Edited by Harold Adams Small. Berkeley: University of California Press, 1939.

Stern, Philip Van Doren. *An End to Valor: The Last Days of the Civil War*. Boston: Houghton Mifflin Company, 1958.

Wecter, Dixon. *When Johnny Comes Marching Home*. Boston: Houghton Mifflin Company, 1944.

Wesley, Charles H. *Negro Americans in the Civil War: From Slavery to Citizenship*. New York: Publishers Company, 1967.

Wiley, Bell Irvin. *The Life of Johnny Reb: The Common Soldier of the Confederacy*. New York: The Bobbs-Merrill Company, 1943.

——————. *The Life of Billy Yank. The Common Soldier of the Union*. New York: The Bobbs-Merrill Company, 1951.

Wood, William Nathaniel. *Reminiscences of Big I*. Jackson, Tenn.: McCowat-Mercer Press, 1956.

Wormeley, Katharine Prescott. *The Cruel Side of War with the Army of the Potomac*. Boston: Roberts Brothers, 1898.

Index

Page numbers in *italics* refer to illustrations

Picture Credits

The photographs in this book are from the following sources and are used with their permission:

Chicago Historical Society • page 44

Clements Library, University of Michigan, Ann Arbor, Mich. • page 27

Eleanor S. Brockenbrough Library, The Museum of the Confederacy, Richmond, Va. • page 47

J. B. Leib Photography Co., York, Pa. • pages 72, 84-85

Library of Congress, Washington, D.C. • pages 3, 5, 8, 11, 13, 15, 16, 19, 21, 23, 24, 25, 26, 29, 32, 41, 45, 55, 57, 59, 61, 63, 67, 68, 71, 76-77, 79, 80, 86, 87, 88, 91, 93

National Archives, Washington, D.C. • pages ii, 36-37, 39, 48, 53, 64

The Seventh Regiment Fund, Inc., New York, N.Y. • page x

U.S. Army Military History Institute, Carlisle Barracks, Pa. • page 83